Applied Psychology
for Social Work

Applied Psychology for Social Work

Second Edition

EWAN INGLEBY

Series Editors: Jonathan Parker and Greta Bradley

LearningMatters

First published in 2006 by Learning Matters Ltd.
Reprinted in 2007
Reprinted in 2008
Second edition 2010

British Library Cataloguing in Publication Data
A CIP record for this book is available from the British Library.

ISBN: 978 1 84445 356 6

Cover and text design by Code 5 Design Associates
Project management by Deer Park Productions
Typeset by Pantek Arts Ltd, Maidstone, Kent
Printed and bound in Great Britain by Bell & Bain Ltd, Glasgow

Learning Matters Ltd
33 Southernhay East
Exeter EX1 1NX
Tel: 01392 215560
info@learningmatters.co.uk
www.learningmatters.co.uk

Mixed Sources
Product group from well-managed
forests and other controlled sources
www.fsc.org Cert no. TT-COC-002769
© 1996 Forest Stewardship Council
FSC

Contents

Acknowledgements

I would like to thank colleagues and students at New College Durham and Teeside University for their contribution to the debates and discussions that have contributed to this book. I would also like to thank Professors John Fulton of Surrey University and John Davis of All Souls College Oxford for encouraging me to persevere with reconciling studying, writing, teaching and administrating. I also need to thank the staff at Learning Matters, particularly Kate Lodge, Di Page and Jonathan Parker for their patience and developmental comments. I am particularly grateful for the support of my parents and my wife Karen and children Bernadette, Teresa and Michael. Without them tomorrow would always be a much harder day.

Introduction

This book has been written for student social workers needing to study and apply psychology to their own practice. Although psychology is typically studied in the first year of the degree programme as a separate module it is a subject that links to much of the rest of the academic curriculum. It is a subject that makes an especially important contribution to understanding human growth and development. Applying psychological therapies to social work can be a way of raising standards and ensuring good practice. This objective is as relevant today as it ever has been. As Mithran Samuel (2006) observes about social work in general, *social care professionals are becoming overwhelmed by paperwork at the expense of working with service-users* (online: www.communitycare.co.uk).

If the centrality of the service user experience is lost it can mean that social work becomes akin to a bureaucratic exercise, what Michelle Binfield (2006) phrases as:

A lack of understanding and an unwillingness to address a multiplicity of needs (online: www.communitycare.co.uk).

This is the reason why this book discusses the application of psychology to social care. It may be argued that of all the social science modules available to social workers psychology is especially important because it offers potential explanations of complex aspects of human behaviour and development. According to the Department of Health it is imperative that human growth and development is taught to all social workers. This recommendation can be put into effect upon realising that psychological therapies can be used with service-users who have many differing needs. My own realisation of this important point occurred when working with service-users with mental health needs and learning disabilities. I had previously studied academic psychology and enjoyed interpreting aspects of my own personality in relation to the textbook psychological theories. This interest was put into perspective upon experiencing the ways in which service-user behaviour can be influenced through the application of psychological therapies. Like many social workers I wanted to go into the profession to help those in need of being helped. On reflection, the experience of care planning through applying psychological therapies to particular service-users was one of the most satisfying aspects of residential social work. It is a memory that will always stay with me. It is one of the reasons for producing this book. A major aim is to convey the idea that applying psychology to social work can make professional practice much more effective. Applying psychology to social work can become a means whereby a balance is offered between what is intrapersonal and particular to the social worker alongside what is interpersonal and accepted as being general good practice between social workers. This means that social psychology is especially important within this book and is discussed in relation to each of the main chapters.

Requirements for social work education

Social work education has undergone significant changes since the introduction of the BA (Hons) programme. An important emphasis is placed upon improving the quality of professional social work training so that service-user needs can be met as fully as possible. This book aims to identify and analyse ways of applying psychology to social care in relation to the National Occupational Standards (NOS) set for social workers. These standards emphasise the priority of working effectively with individuals, families, carers, groups and communities in order to raise life opportunities. Six key roles are identified by the standards as contributing to the key purpose of social work:

- preparing for and working with individuals, families, carers, groups and communities;
- planning, carrying out, reviewing and evaluating social work practice;
- supporting individuals to represent their needs, views and circumstances;
- managing risk to individuals, families, carers, groups, communities, self and colleagues;
- managing and being accountable, with supervision and support for social work practice within individual organisations;
- demonstrating professional competence in social work practice.

Book structure

This book concentrates on applying psychology to social work practice. In each of the chapters there are formative activities that attempt to develop cognitive skills so that as well as identifying how social work can be applied to social care, there is academic analysis alongside synthesis in relation to one's own experience in social work.

An important theme of the book is to emphasise the importance of social workers viewing psychology in relation to social care. This means that psychological therapies are particularly important for social workers. The ideas are of most use when they are applied to particular contexts of social care. This is why all of the chapters in the book contain activities that aim to apply psychology to particular social work contexts. These activities attempt to engage the reader with the concept that for social workers psychology ought not to be thought of in isolation from contexts of social care.

The book's chapters focus upon six main aspects of psychology in relation to social care. The first chapter outlines some of the key psychological perspectives that have influenced social care. There is an overview of behaviourism, humanism and psychodynamic, cognitive and biological perspectives. From the beginning of the book there is exemplification in order to show the therapies that are available for social work. As well as identifying the important ideas of each of the perspectives, there is analysis of the strengths and weaknesses of each of the perspectives as well as a critical appraisal of the effectiveness of the therapies that have their basis in each of the perspectives. These psychological perspectives are appraised in relation to a range of social work and social care roles, tasks and settings.

In 2002, the General Social Care Council (GSCC) emphasised the importance of effective communication within social work. Indeed the Department of Health considers that one of the ways to improve the communication skills of social workers is to have a compulsory social work qualification. This reiterates some of the main recommendations that resulted from the inquiries into the deaths of Maria Colwell and Victoria Climbié. This is why Chapter 2 explores some of the psychological explanations of how and why we communicate. After identifying the different forms of communication there follows analysis of the forms of communication. This analysis is designed to place into perspective the interaction of service-users and social workers.

Chapter 3 focuses upon psychology, attitudes and beliefs. The chapter discusses how and why particular attitudes and beliefs are formed. There is an explanation of how and why social stereotypes are formed with discussion of the subsequent impact of discrimination against particular groups within society.

All of the main chapters within the book are designed to focus upon key areas of social work practice. Chapter 4 discusses the contributions psychology has made to the interpretation of mental illness. The chapter develops the theme that effective social work practice necessitates being aware of the advantages and disadvantages of the therapies available to service-users who have been diagnosed as having mental illness.

Chapter 5 discusses the contribution made by psychology to understanding the growth and development of children. Psychology is a subject that in general makes an excellent contribution to understanding human development. For social workers wanting to specialise in working with children this chapter provides information that assists us in understanding the psychological factors impacting upon child development.

Chapter 6 identifies and analyses the contribution that psychology makes to gerontology. It is essential that social workers are able to identify the inaccuracy of negative social stereotypes so this chapter presents psychological research findings that identify the reality of the ageing process as opposed to focusing upon perceptions of reality.

The book attempts to provide a comprehensive coverage of psychology in relation to social work. As opposed to being a general psychology textbook it is specifically written for the social work degree programme and attempts to combine practical social work experience alongside sound academic analysis.

Learning features

The book attempts to stimulate learning through interactive activities. As well as these activities there are case study examples and research tasks. The book aims to develop your analytical skills so that there is a creative engagement with the content and the application of skills of critical appraisal. Through completing these learning activities your individual experience of social care contexts can be applied to particular psychological issues and concerns. Alongside the interactive learning activities there are supporting references so that your knowledge of psychology in relation to social care can be synthesised in relation to these texts.

Professional development and reflective practice

A major aim of the new social work qualification is to provide social care professionals who are able to reflect on social work practice. This book attempts to facilitate self-analysis in relation to psychology and social care. From this self-reflection there is the possibility of development in relation to meeting complex service-user needs. If this aim is realised it will help to achieve some of the laudable aims of the National Occupational Standards, the General Social Care Council and the Department of Health.

Chapter 1
Introducing social workers to psychology

ACHIEVING A SOCIAL WORK DEGREE

This chapter will begin to help you to meet the following National Occupational Standards:

Key Role 1: Prepare for and work with individuals, families, carers, groups and communities to assess their needs and circumstances.

- Prepare for social work contact and involvement.
- Assess needs and options to recommend a course of action.

Key Role 2: Plan, carry out, review and evaluate social work practice with individuals, families, carers, groups, communities and other professionals.

- Respond to crisis situations.
- Interact with individuals, families, carers, groups and communities to achieve change and development and to improve life opportunities.
- Address behaviour which presents a risk to individuals, families, carers, groups and communities.

Key Role 5: Manage and be accountable with supervision and support for your own social work practice within your own organisation.

- Manage and be accountable for your own work.
- Work within multidisciplinary and multi-organisational teams, networks and systems.

Key Role 6: Demonstrate professional competence in social work practice.

- Research, analyse, evaluate and use current knowledge of best social work practice.
- Contribute to the promotion of best social work practice.

It will also introduce you to the following academic standards as set out in the social work subject benchmark statement:

3.1.4 Social work theory

Research-based concepts and critical explanations from social work theory and other disciplines that contribute to the knowledge base of social work including their distinctive epistemological status and application to practice.

3.1.5 The nature of social work practice

The factors and processes that facilitate effective interdisciplinary, interprofessional and interagency collaboration and partnership.

The subject skills highlighted to demonstrate this knowledge in practice include:

- Assess human situations, taking into account a variety of factors.
- Assess the merits of contrasting theories, explanations, research, policies and procedures.

In this opening chapter there is an introduction to the discipline of psychology and discussion of how psychology can be applied to social work. Each school of psychology has a different understanding of what constitutes the self. This understanding is explained, analysed and critically appraised within the chapter. Throughout this introductory chapter there are formative activities that reinforce learning in relation to the main psychological paradigms that are of relevance for social workers.

After reading this chapter you should be able to:

- identify what the term 'psychology' means;

- analyse some of the ways that psychology can be used by social workers;

- critically appraise some of the ways that psychology can be applied to social work.

It can be argued that psychology may be visualised as an academic 'ship of fools'. Like the famous Hieronymus Bosch painting, the subject is similar to a boat that is at times unsure of its direction, with competing views on which course ought to be followed. This chapter explores some of the influential perspectives that have influenced psychology and ultimately shaped its form as an academic discipline. Before we look at the main psychological perspectives and discuss how social workers can apply psychological ideas it is important to begin at the beginning and identify what is meant by the term 'psychology'.

The discipline of psychology

'Psychology' is not as simplistic to define as it might initially appear. It is more than just a word. To a layperson an immediate reaction may be to associate psychology with 'reading people's minds' or 'analysing aspects of human behaviour'. A dictionary definition of psychology may give a precise explanation but this precision can disguise the complexity of the subject. An example dictionary definition is that psychology can be understood as being *the scientific study of all forms of human and animal behaviour*.

ACTIVITY 1.1

Take a few minutes here to think about what you understand by this dictionary definition. Is it similar or different to your understanding of the word psychology? How is it similar? How does it differ?

COMMENT

Although this is an accurate definition of what psychology is, it does not acknowledge the many competing theories of how and why one should study and apply psychology. It is a definition that alludes to the complexity of studying the vast range of human and animal behaviour but one that does not explain the differing perspectives in relation to why particular forms of behaviour occur. We need to take into account this dictionary definition and then add depth and layers of meaning to the literal definition of psychology.

If we develop this initial understanding of what psychology is we can assert that psychologists are not mind-readers and they do not necessarily have access to our thoughts. They do not work solely with people who are mentally ill or people who are emotionally disturbed. These are common delusions and misinterpretations of the discipline.

To go back to the beginning, the word psychology is derived from two Greek words 'psyche' (or mind) and 'logos' (or study). This means that psychology literally translates as the study of the mind. Malim and Birch (1998) claim that the discipline began in 1879 when Wilhelm Wundt opened the first psychology laboratory at the University of Leipzig in Germany. Wundt focused upon 'introspection', or observing and analysing the structure of conscious mental processes. It was the emphasis placed upon measurement and control that marked the separation of psychology from its parent discipline philosophy.

It can be argued that by 1920 the usefulness of this method was questioned. John B Watson was one of a number of theorists who believed that it was wrong to focus upon introspection because this approach to studying psychology cannot be measured. Consequently Watson dedicated himself to the study of what has become known as 'behaviourism', or what is measurable and observable. Behaviourism remained the dominant force in psychology over the next 30 years, especially in the USA. The emphasis was placed upon identifying the external factors that produce learning or conditioning, the stimuli producing responses.

As with many philosophical and sociological perspectives, psychology is characterised by competing paradigms or models of thought, with theorists becoming grouped together according to which perspective they are representing. Malim and Birch (1998) argue that an interesting reaction to behaviourism came in the form of the Gestalt school of psychology emerging in Austria and Germany in the 1920s and popularised by Fritz Perls. This branch of psychology suggests that the whole is greater than its parts and that this in turn complicates a focus upon the external factors producing thoughts. In other words there is no one psychological perspective that holds all the answers in relation to defining the discipline.

A further criticism of behaviourism developed through the twentieth century as a result of the legacy of Sigmund Freud (who has become possibly the most famous psychologist). Freud proposed that the mind is a combination of conscious and unconscious thoughts. If this is the case the theory can be used to challenge behaviourism because it means that human thought and behaviour is more complex than the behaviourist notion that external variables create thought and behaviour. If, for example, we do not know why we have dreams how can we make a simplistic claim that they have been produced by external variables?

Alongside this influential psychological perspective, there emerged a further significant theory that placed its emphasis upon thinking processes or cognition, in other words the ways in which we attain, retain and regain information. Within this perspective it is what happens after a stimulus but before a response that becomes the main psychological focus. The mind is seen as being like an information-processor, almost akin to a computer. Malim and Birch (1998, p25) explain this perspective by arguing that *human beings are seen as information processors who absorb information from the outside world, code and interpret it, store and retrieve it*. This could lead back to the initial criticism of introspection being unlikely to explain the complexity of human thought so it could be argued that things have come back full circle in a literal revolution of thought.

This point is reinforced by some of the current developments within psychology. The scientific advances of the 1990s and beyond in relation to identifying the genetic and hormonal composition of the human mind have generated enormous interest in the idea that thoughts and behaviour are determined by our biology. Once again it can be suggested that this is a reductionist argument. It reduces complex thoughts and behaviour to a few variables such as hormones and genes. It may prove to be yet another passing paradigm contributing to the discipline of psychology that will be criticised and revised with the benefit of academic analysis.

From this initial debate about what is meant by the word psychology we can ask a further question in relation to the nature of the human mind. Is the human mind the same as the human brain?

ACTIVITY *1.2*

Think about the above question. Can it be argued that the mind is the same as the brain? If so, why? If not, why not?

COMMENT

One answer to this question is that there is no definite answer. Theorists have speculated for hundreds, if not thousands, of years about what has come to be known as 'the mind–brain problem'. Whether one focuses upon the mind or the brain depends upon the understanding of how psychology should be studied. It may be argued that many of the social psychological perspectives such as behaviourism and humanism and psychodynamic and cognitive theories emphasise the importance of the mind whereas biological perspectives are more likely to place an emphasis upon the genes and hormones influencing the brain.

We can now look at exploring some of these understandings of psychology. This is a way of adding detail to our introductory explanations of what the subject is. It is a means of setting the scene before we analyse how psychology can be applied to social work.

The schools of psychology

Table 1.1 provides a summary of five major schools of psychology together with a brief description of their key features. This initial table is then developed to identify some critical features of each of the psychological perspectives in relation to key terminology and influential psychologists.

Table 1.1 *Schools of psychology*

School	Key features
Behaviourism	Human behaviour is seen as being shaped by environmental forces and is a collection of learned responses to external stimuli. The key learning process is known as 'conditioning'.
Humanism	The individual is seen as being unique, rational and self-determining. Present experience is held to be as important as past experience.
Psychodynamic theory	The mind is seen as being a combination of conscious thoughts and the workings of the unconscious mind. The unconscious mind expresses itself through dreams and behaviour we are not consciously aware of.
Cognitive theory	This perspective looks at what happens after a stimulus but before a response. The human mind is likened to a computer. People are seen as information processors, selecting, coding, storing and retrieving information when needed.
Neurobiological theory	Behaviour is considered as being determined by genetic, physiological and neurobiological factors and processes.

These schools of thought are especially important because of the influence they have had in shaping the academic concerns of psychology. Their origins go back to some of the earliest philosophical ideas to have influenced western thought. It may be suggested that the proposition that there are forces beyond the individual that shape social reality goes back to the ideas of the Greek philosopher Plato. This idea is central to behaviourism so it can be proposed that the perspective has its intellectual origins in this classical thought. It may also be proposed that the notion that individuals interpret their social world as opposed to being ultimately shaped by this world goes back to the ideas of Aristotle. This philosophy is of central importance to humanism. In other words the genesis of the perspective's dominant idea can be traced back to these early times.

There follows a summary of each of the key perspectives that develops those definitions given in Table 1.1. Each of the key perspectives is defined, key figures influencing the perspective are identified and central terms within each perspective are explained.

Behaviourism

Behaviourists emphasise the importance of external factors producing thoughts within the human mind. A key behaviourist idea is that every individual enters the world as a 'clean slate'. The surrounding environment is considered to be the 'chalk' etching its marks upon the 'slate' of the mind. This means that the individual enters the world without a fixed identity and that social factors are responsible for making the individual whosoever he or she becomes. The Jesuit notion of 'give me the boy and I'll show you the man' equates to this idea. This suggests that we become who we are as a result of factors beyond and outside individuals.

A number of psychologists have become famous members of the behaviourist school of thought. Burrhus Skinner, Edward Thorndike, John Watson and Ivan Pavlov have become synonymous with behaviourist psychology. All of these psychologists share in common the belief that external factors are of critical importance in producing thoughts and behaviour.

The terms 'classical conditioning' and 'operant conditioning' are particularly important within behaviourism. Classical conditioning is associated with the work of Ivan Pavlov. It has become associated with the ways whereby biological responses are regulated by external factors. This produces what has become phrased as a 'conditioned response' where a form of behaviour occurs in association with a particular stimulus. Operant conditioning is a term that has become associated with the work of Burrhus Skinner. It refers to the link that exists between positively affirming behaviour that reinforces a particular stimulus. To give a simple example, if a child responds favourably to a parental instruction the child is usually praised. This reinforcement of learning through praise is therefore a type of operant conditioning. In the following case study there is the exemplification of when humans may experience classical and operant conditioning.

CASE STUDY

Sophie is four years old and she has just started school. She has been in the school for one month and she has already learned many of the school rules. She has noticed that when the school bell rings at 9 a.m. she has to line up with all the other children and stand still with her arms by her side looking out for her class teacher Mrs Black. At first a number of the infants did not know what to do when the bell rang at the start of the school day. The sight of all the other children moving into line upset some of the infants as they felt afraid and anxious because they did not know what they were supposed to do. This association of the bell ringing and anxiety has gradually made the infants copy what the other children were doing. Today when the bell rang at 9 a.m. nearly all of the infants copied the other older children so that they would not stand out and feel anxious. They got into line standing with their arms by their sides looking out for Mrs Black. They moved a little bit more than the other older children but their response to the bell ringing at 9 a.m. has become conditioned into acceptable behaviour. On Friday Sophie received the headmaster's award for her good work. She felt very proud as she had to go onto the stage at assembly and receive a gold badge. All the other children clapped when her name was read out and she received her badge from the head teacher. Sophie remembered her parents' words that in school she should always try her hardest.

Humanism

Humanism does acknowledge the importance of environmental factors on the mind but it places an emphasis upon individual interpretation of external factors. This means that, as opposed to emphasising the importance of external variables, attention is given to the importance of individuals interpreting social reality. Humanism can be associated with the philosophy of Immanuel Kant and his 'Copernican revolution' of thought (Audi, 1995, p400). As opposed to asking about the reality of the universe, Kant changes the focus of the argument to ask about how individuals understand social reality. Humanism asks a similar question. In contrast to focusing upon how external variables produce thoughts, the humanist emphasis is on how individuals make sense of external variables.

Humanism has become associated with the work of Carl Rogers and Abraham Maslow. Maslow proposes that all humans have a 'hierarchy of needs' and that individual thoughts are influenced by the extent to which these physiological and intellectual needs are being met. Carl Rogers has had a particularly important influence on humanism and it may be claimed that Rogers is the founding father of psychological humanism. His work is also influential in what is considered as being effective social work practice. One of the most important Rogerian ideas to have influenced social care is the proposal that anxiety is a product of what has become termed as a 'would/should dilemma'. This means that an individual wants to do something but they are unable to achieve this wish. According to Rogers this then generates tension within the individual that in turn produces anxiety.

In applying therapy to resolve the would/should dilemma, Rogers recommends that the therapist must have a congruent or genuine interest in the service-user. This means that empathy is a central concept to the Rogerian model of client-centred therapy. The ideal aim is to lead the service-user to his/her 'inner beautiful self' so that the individual's would/should dilemma can be overcome.

ACTIVITY *1.3*

Think about your own personal development. To what extent do you think that your personality has been formed as a result of external environmental factors? To what extent do you think that your personality is a product of your unique personality?

COMMENT

Most people would probably accept that their personality is a combination of external environmental variables alongside their own unique personal traits. In other words the person is a product of factors that are both outside and inside the individual. It is interesting, however, to consider why and when the emphasis placed upon the individual and the environment varies. In this country particular social, economic and religious variables have influenced the extent to which one's surroundings or one's personality are held accountable for personality development. In the UK there are many communities that emphasise self-responsibility. If one claims that the environment is responsible for personal development this may be regarded as an attempt to disown one's accountability for individual life circumstances. Some of the popular movements of the 1960s and 1970s may have changed this perception but the prevailing thought in the UK today would seem to be that individual characteristics are especially important in determining one's personality. This may lessen the importance of the behaviourist perspective and make humanism a more influential explanation of individual circumstances.

Psychodynamic theory

Psychodynamic psychology is associated with the ideas of one of the most famous psychologists, Sigmund Freud. Freud's theory postulates that thoughts are a product of the working of both the conscious and the unconscious mind (Gross, 1999, p969). We have conscious thoughts that we are aware of and unconscious thoughts that appear in our mind in the form of dreams. Moreover, what happens in our conscious mind in turn influences what thoughts filter through to our unconscious mind.

Freud considers that there are three especially important components to every individual (Gross, 1999, p591). There is the 'id' or biological physiology of maleness and femaleness. There is the 'ego' or social self to regulate our biological 'id'. There is also the 'superego' existing beyond the individual that generates a common understanding of our social identity.

Freud claims that all individuals go through a number of stages of development. From 0–1 a child is considered to be in an oral stage of development. This means that the infant is preoccupied with its mouth. This then leads to the anal stage of development from 1–2 when the infant becomes aware of its capacity to excrete and urinate. The next developmental stage is the phallic stage of development when boys and girls become increasingly aware of physical maleness and femaleness. Freud claims that this occurs between the ages of 3 and 6 resulting in a close relationship between a boy and his mother and a girl and her father. After the phallic stage of development there is what Freud terms as a latent phase of development. This occurs between the ages of 6 and 12 as the individual becomes more concerned with their social identity as they become increasingly aware of their ego state. The theory states that the final stage of development is the genital stage from the age of 12 onwards when Freud proposes that males and females become increasingly aware of their adult reproductive capabilities.

Freud's theory introduces the idea that human beings hold the potential for fixated behaviour. This means that an individual could become negatively confined to a particular stage (or stages) of development. As an example, if an infant experienced the trauma of losing its mother at the age of 1, there is the possibility of this individual developing what Freud terms an 'oral fixation'. This fixated behaviour expresses itself at a later age through consciously chosen behaviour exemplified by the oral fixation of alcoholism. What makes the theory so original is that it is claimed that the conscious choice of behaviour has its origins in the repressed depths of the unconscious mind. Proponents of the theory claim that this repression can be released through psychodynamic counselling. This counselling may be needed in a situation when the individual has experienced a physical and/or emotional crisis during their development.

Crises leading to fixated behaviour can occur at any stage of development. According to Freud this personal development directs the individual in the direction of one of two forces, either towards 'thanatos' or 'eros'. Eros, the Greek god of love, is interpreted by Freudians as contributing to an individual's optimism. Thanatos, the Greek personification of death, is perceived as contributing to an individual's sense of pessimism. How one develops determines whether one's conscious frame of mind directs the individual to the good or otherwise. It can be argued that Freud's legacy is to have left one of the most influential psychological theories to contribute to the discipline. It is, however, important to recognise that just because the theory is famous does not mean it is correct. This point will be developed later in the chapter.

Cognitive theory

Cognitive psychology can be understood as being a branch of psychology that is interested in what happens after a stimulus but before a response. It is a school of psychology that has become associated with the work of Jean Piaget and Lev Vygotsky. Malim and

Birch (1998, p27) argue that Piaget is *the most significant figure in the study of cognitive development*. Piaget's model of cognitive development has become particularly influential within psychology. According to Piaget the human mind develops over time as an individual is stimulated by its surroundings. From the ages of 0–2 the child has basic thoughts or 'schemata'. Piaget claims that these initial thoughts are limited and instinctive. A baby has a 'crying schema', a 'grasping schema' and a 'feeding schema'. These thought processes develop from the age of 2 as the infant becomes capable of speech and develops what Piaget phrases as 'symbolic thought'. It is also proposed that between the ages of 2 and 7 the child's problem-solving skills are limited because of two terms Piaget phrases as 'centration' and 'egocentricism'. By 'centration' Piaget means that the child can see one aspect of a situation's reality but not the total picture. As an example, a child between the ages of 2 and 7 may think that a ton of lead is heavier than a ton of feathers because they 'centrate' or focus on one aspect of the problem. The child assumes that lead is a metal and therefore heavier than 'fluffy' feathers. This means that the child may not see that in fact both quantities are the same weight. By 'egocentrism' Piaget means that a child cannot see the true nature of a problem because problem solving occurs in relation to what the child knows about reality. As an example, if a child aged 2–7 is asked what noise a reindeer makes it may say 'clip clop' instead of 'I don't know'. This is due to egocentrism. The child thinks that the reindeer looks like a horse and knows that a horse makes a 'clip clop' sound so it assumes that reindeer also make a 'clip clop' sound. Piaget claims that in order to progress through this stage of development the child needs to interact with its environment through play.

As a consequence of linguistic development the infant becomes capable of more complex thought so that by the age of 7 the preoperational stage has ended and the child is able to complete complex problem solving. This stage of development is phrased 'concrete operations'. This is because Piaget claims that children aged between 7 and 11 need to use props if they are to complete problem-solving activities. From 7–11 a child can calculate that 3 apples plus 2 apples add up to make 5 apples but Piaget claims that the child needs to have the actual apples to hand in order to complete the calculation. As this interaction occurs the child will develop what Piaget phrases as 'reversible thinking'. This is the final stage of cognitive development occurring around 11 years of age. Once reversible thought has been reached it is possible to problem solve within the mind, without using the props that a seven-year-old child needs. When one can apply reversible thinking to solving a problem, it means that one can see within one's mind that $3 + 2$ is the same as $7 - 2$.

Lev Vygotsky's work is seen as complementing Piaget's theory rather than being a radically different cognitive perspective (Malim and Birch, 1998, p469). Vygotsky places more emphasis upon the social factors influencing the child's cognitive development. One of Vygotsky's central ideas is the notion of each individual having a 'scaffold' of persons aiding their cognitive development. According to the nature of the scaffold one's cognitive development is affected in either negative or positive ways. If, for example, one's peers are interested in academic issues, this social scaffold will impact upon the individual's cognitive development and make the individual more academic. If the opposite situation occurs it leads to negative cognitive development. It can be argued that this theory complements Piaget's work because it explains why some individuals are 'late developers' and reach the stage of reversible thought beyond the age of 11. Vygotsky uses the term 'ZPD' or 'Zone of Proximal Development' to refer to when an individual has fulfilled their cognitive potential. This stage of development may occur at 11. It may occur beyond the age of 11. What becomes critical is the influence of one's cognitive development in relation to the 'scaffold' of individuals influencing one's cognitive development.

Biological psychology

It can be argued that biological psychology is becoming of increasing importance due to the recent scientific advances in particular in relation to understanding human genetics. The biological perspective places an emphasis on the link between the thoughts of individuals and their hormonal and chromosomal composition. It is accepted by the scientific community that males and females differ in one pair of chromosomes and that before the infant is born the presence of a 'Y' chromosome leads to the development of testes. This in turn leads to the production of the hormone testosterone. As a consequence males produce more androgens whereas females produce oestrogen and progesterone. Biologists such as Milton Diamond and Roger Gorski emphasise the importance of biology in producing thoughts. It has been discovered that the male brain is physically different to the female brain due to the influence of the hormone testosterone. According to this theory the inevitable consequence is that the thoughts occurring within the mind must have some biological basis and that differences in thought patterns are crucially linked to hormonal and chromosomal factors.

Applying psychology to social work

All of the psychological perspectives that have been introduced within this chapter can be applied to the everyday practice of a social worker. There exist a number of psychological therapies and each one has the potential to improve and enhance a social worker's professional practice. Moreover, if the therapies are combined they offer the potential to give holistic therapy in order to assist service-users with multiple needs. This next section of the chapter introduces some of the therapies that are available for social work service-users.

Behaviourist therapies

One of the most well-known behaviourist therapies is called 'token economy'. The therapy is based on the principle of conditioning the service-users' responses, effectively manipulating choice so that positive behaviour occurs. Most humans have complex thoughts and choose whether to conform with or rebel against accepted social requirements. This acceptance or rebellion can be overt and explicit or implicit and assumed. Token economy attempts to produce conformity of response. At the end of every day in which the individual has complied with what is required a reward or 'token' is given to the service-user. This token has to have appeal and value to the service-user. If there is a lack of compliance with the programme the token is denied to the service-user. After a certain duration, for example five days of compliance, the service-user is rewarded with a bigger treat or prize. Token economy is used within many primary schools. It is a behaviourist attempt to get children to comply with what is required of them within the school environment. It is a therapy that is also used within other social work contexts, but as we shall see later in the chapter, it is a therapy that is not without its critics.

Another therapy that is available for social work service-users is biofeedback. This therapy is used typically with those people who have been referred for professional help because they are highly anxious. Music, light, aroma and relaxing furnishings are combined to produce an environment that can physically relax the individual. The therapy is essentially attempting to produce relaxing thoughts within the service-user's mind by manipulating external variables.

A third popular therapy that has its origins within behaviourist theory is known as 'systematic desensitisation'. This therapy is used with service-users who have phobias. The service-user is made to come to terms with his or her phobia in a controlled environment. It is proposed that as a result of gradually exposing the individual to the phobia in a non-threatening way, the phobic object becomes manageable and increasingly less debilitating. Once again the emphasis is placed upon the importance of the psychologist manipulating the individual's thoughts in order to produce positive ways of thinking about the phobia. The following case study example outlines the ways in which behaviourism can be applied to social work. It also reveals some of the potential difficulties that exist when particular therapies are applied to service-users who have particular needs.

CASE STUDY

James lives in residential care. He is 27 and has learning disabilities but there has been no definitive diagnosis of the nature of his disability. He is thought to have a combination of autism and learning disability. Before James goes to sleep at night he has a habit of getting all of his shoes from his wardrobe and throwing them down the stairs. In an attempt to get James to change his behaviour his social worker has devised a token economy programme in conjunction with other members of the multidisciplinary team who work with him. James loves dance music and it is proposed to give him a token on each day when he does not throw his shoes down the stairs. James collects coins and on each day when he has complied with the care programme he is given a coin of his choice. If he does not follow what is expected of him James is denied a coin. Upon receiving five coins, James is given the opportunity to go into town with his social worker and choose a dance record of his choice. Once James understood how the programme was meant to work his behaviour changed and he no longer gets his shoes from his wardrobe in order to throw them down the stairs at the end of the day.

Although James's social worker is impressed with the care programme, some of the other staff in the office have expressed concerns that there are ethical problems with this behaviour modification programme. It is emphasised that James is 27 and there are worries that this conditioning violates his right to choose what he should and should not do.

Humanist therapies

It can be argued that many understandings of what constitutes good social work practice is in effect putting the ideas of Carl Rogers into practice. Rogers proposed an egalitarian model of therapy in which the therapist is not above the service-user but 'with' the service-user. Empathy is a particularly important aspect of the Rogerian way. The therapist must be there for his or her service-user and prepared to be genuine and assertive. According to Rogers it is only through the occurrence of genuine counselling that an individual's problems can be resolved.

Therapy focuses on resolving the would/should dilemma that is the cause of the anxiety that has led to the service-user needing therapy. The therapist is also attempting to direct the individual to his or her 'beautiful inner self'. Rogers believed that all individuals are innately good and that it is only the tension that results from a would/should dilemma that makes the individual a less than good person. Through a counselling relationship that is genuine and empathetic it is postulated that the would/should dilemma will be replaced by an assertive awareness of one's inner goodness. Although there are many applications for this type of therapy, the generalising assumptions that are made within humanism can mean that its application is restricted. This argument is exemplified in the following case study example and in the final section of the chapter.

CASE STUDY

Julie has recently qualified as a social worker and she is working with young adults in an inner-city estate. Within the last few months there has been an escalation of racial tension between black and white youths. The situation is further complicated by an outbreak of violence between Asian and Afro-Caribbean youths. As a student Julie was inspired by the ideas of Carl Rogers and she bases her social work counselling upon the principles of client-centred therapy. Within one of her first counselling sessions with a young Asian man, Julie is devastated when her service-user walks out of the session telling Julie that as a young white female she knows 'nothing about what is happening'. Julie realises that her values are very different from the values of her service-user and that this limits the application of client-centred therapy. In the past she has found that this therapy works with single white female service-users who seem to share many of her values but it is an altogether different challenge applying these ideas in this particular context.

Psychodynamic therapies

The psychodynamic model of the mind holds that conscious thoughts are influenced by the unconscious mind. This means that therapy involves releasing what is being unconsciously repressed. This then enables the individual to deal with these thoughts within the conscious mind. The psychodynamic therapist is responsible for interpreting what is within the service-user's unconscious mind by analysing dreams and/or using hypnotherapy. Dream and fantasy analysis become a means of interpreting what is being repressed. It is considered to be imperative for repressed unconscious thoughts to be released into the conscious mind in order to lessen the effects of repression. The Freudian model holds that fixated behaviour has its basis in repression so that the critical role of the therapist is one of releasing repressed thoughts and then recommending ways of consciously dealing with these thoughts.

The psychodynamic model is hierarchical as opposed to being egalitarian. The omniscient therapist is in a position of power over his or her service-users, a characteristic that can be deemed as being opposed to the equalitarian approach of Carl Rogers. This has consequences for the situations in which the therapy can be used and the service-users upon whom the therapy should be used. This critique of psychodynamic therapy is exemplified in the following case study.

CASE STUDY

Catherine has had an eating disorder (anorexia nervosa) since she was 16. She is now 42 and she has never been able to have a permanent relationship. Although she wants to have children she is not able to have a family due to her debilitating eating disorder. Catherine is consciously aware of her eating disorder but she cannot explain why she has this condition. She does not know anyone else in her family who has an eating disorder. Catherine has tried a number of different forms of counselling including Rogerian therapy but the counselling has been unable to help. This led to Catherine paying for psychodynamic counselling. The counselling sessions appeared to help her because they focused on the link existing between Catherine's conscious and unconscious mind. The counsellor explained to Catherine that she was experiencing an oral fixation and that her conscious eating disorder could be traced back to her unconscious mind. Catherine was adopted at birth. It was postulated that Catherine's eating disorder was a consequence of being adopted at birth. Catherine found the counselling most helpful. The counselling sessions led her to contact her natural mother. The subsequent meetings meant that Catherine's conscious thoughts were more positive. This helped in promoting a more positive self perception. Although the therapy worked, Catherine sometimes wondered if her conscious eating disorder could really be traced to a time in her life she couldn't remember. It seemed a bizarre explanation for her conscious thoughts.

Cognitive therapies

Cognitive psychologists emphasise the importance of studying what happens after a stimulus but before a reaction. They are interested in the processes within the mind that produce thoughts, not in a biological sense but in terms of cognitive processes. It is proposed that through manipulating these cognitive processes one's thought processes can change. If, for example, a service-user is unable to control their anger, it may be possible to apply cognitive therapy so that this anger is effectively managed. By counselling the individual to consciously change the thought processes occurring within the mind so that they think differently, there follows a cognitive restructuring. This allows the service-user to think about the world in a different way. It is a therapy relying on psychological techniques as opposed to a medical therapy. If it is combined with other psychological therapies it can offer a potential solution to various psychological problems such as low self-esteem and inability to manage anger. The following case study outlines how cognitive therapy can be applied to a particular example of anger management.

CASE STUDY

Benjamin had always wanted to be an HGV driver and he was delighted to have obtained his licence. It meant that he was able to complete long-haul drives over to Europe and at first he regarded this as his ideal career. After four months of shift work, Benjamin noticed that he was becoming increasingly prone to episodes of road rage. It began with him making private comments about other drivers and it escalated into him making aggressive gestures to drivers Benjamin assumed were not taking due consideration on the road. One incident troubled Benjamin. He thought that a driver had flashed the car lights at him aggressively and Benjamin followed the driver for five miles 'bumper to bumper'. He almost 'shunted' into the car when they reached some traffic lights. Benjamin asked his GP if he could recommend anything to calm his road rage and he was referred to a cognitive behaviourist therapist who began to counsel Benjamin. The therapy seemed to work. Benjamin was taught how to control his anger by controlling his thoughts when he was driving, by thinking in a non-aggressive way. As he was driving, Benjamin was asked to imagine that he had an instructor watching him who could revoke his HGV licence if he showed any signs of road rage. The therapist also recommended that Benjamin should put the office phone number and a sign asking 'Well driven?' at the back of the lorry. The combination of anger management and applied behaviourism seemed to make a dramatic difference to Benjamin's ability to control his temper.

Biological therapies

Biological psychology attempts to understand the human mind by applying traditional western scientific principles. Therapies are based on the idea that thought processes are determined by the genetic and hormonal nature of the brain. It is also proposed that thought processes can be influenced by drug therapy. As an example, an overly aggressive service-user may be diagnosed as being overly aggressive because of the presence of too much testosterone within the body. This male hormone testosterone may need to be regulated by medication that lessens the aggressive impulses that are produced within the mind.

In the application of therapies based upon biological psychology, social workers may be required to monitor the drug therapy of particular service-users. To give an example, it has been discovered that in some instances placing the individual on a drug regime based on dopamine can regulate schizophrenia. If levels of dopamine within the brain determine the presence or otherwise of schizophrenic tendencies it can be argued that drug therapies have their value within social work. It may also be argued that the precise link between the chemical composition of the brain and thought processes has never been exactly established and that this psychological perspective has not developed as yet to the extent that it can offer every possible solution for every possible psychological need.

ACTIVITY *1.4*

Think about each of the schools of psychology outlined in Table 1.1 and suggest how they might explain why individuals drink excessive amounts of alcohol and how individuals could be induced to stop excessive drinking.

COMMENT

Each of the psychological schools of thought would answer the question differently. Behaviourist psychologists think that the external environment shapes the individual. This means that excessive drinking is considered to be a form of learned behaviour. The way to change the behaviour is to offer an incentive to stop excessive drinking through systems of reward and punishment. If an individual associates drinking with negative thoughts and not drinking with positive thoughts it is proposed that they are likely to stop abusing alcohol. Humanists such as Carl Rogers would interpret excessive drinking as being a sign of anxiety. Anxiety is a product of what Rogers describes as a 'would/should' dilemma, in other words an individual is not able to do what they would like to do. Resolve this dilemma and they are likely to stop drinking. Psychoanalysts consider that conscious thoughts are influenced by what is within the unconscious mind. Drinking is considered to be a conscious fixation resulting from a repressed unconscious experience. It may be postulated that when the individual was a baby they had a traumatic experience during their oral stage of development and that the conscious act of drinking is a means of releasing this repressed thought. The way to resolve this fixation is to have psychodynamic counselling whereby the counsellor can help the individual to resolve the conflict between unconscious and conscious thoughts. Neurobiological psychologists explain behaviour through analysing an individual's genetic composition. The implication is that heavy drinkers are more likely to be genetically disposed to alcohol addiction. The way to stop drinking would be to isolate and amend the biological gene promoting this behaviour. At present this procedure is talked about as opposed to being done. Cognitive psychologists would explain drinking as being part of an individual's cognitive map or thinking processes. It is a type of behaviour that comes from within the mind. In order to stop individuals drinking it is proposed that one needs to have a cognitive restructuring of the individual's thinking processes via cognitive counselling.

RESEARCH ACTIVITY

When you do your social work placements take a research diary and make a note of which therapies are being applied to the service-users you meet. Analyse the effectiveness of the therapies by identifying which therapies work and why you think they are working.

We can now complete our introductory chapter by focusing our discussion on critically appraising the psychological perspectives in terms of their value for social work.

Critical appraisal of how psychological therapies can be used by social workers

There is no single perspective that holds all the answers to solving the complex problems faced by many service-users needing social work care. Human beings are complex and although they have needs which are shared in common with others, the interpretation of needs can be particular to the individual. This means that the psychological therapies that have been outlined have limited application.

The behaviourist therapies that have been summarised can make the mistake of focusing upon external variables to such an extent that the particular needs of individuals are not met. Every human being does not react in the same way to an external response. Even complex mammals such as dolphins can defy the laws of operant conditioning by doing the opposite to what they are expected to do. This means that there can be no scientific certainty of the therapies that are informed by this perspective.

There is a further difficulty with behaviourist therapies that may be summarised as being linked to the unique nature of the human mind. There are profound ethical difficulties with therapies such as token economy. If a social worker were to put older service-users on a token economy programme it could be claimed that the dignity and human rights of the individuals are not being respected. A token economy programme is essentially saying 'do this for me and you will be rewarded'. This is a power relationship and it could be argued that the individual is being manipulated in a hierarchical non-egalitarian way. This means that there are critiques of behaviourist therapies and concerns that they have limited application to social care. It leads Malim and Birch (1998, p24) to criticise behaviourist therapies because they can be *mechanistic* and that they *overlook the realm of consciousness and subjective experience*.

It can also be proposed that there are limitations in the application of Rogerian client-centred therapy. For the service-user to accept the importance of resolving the would/should dilemma it is important that they share values similar to those of the therapist. The service-user needs to accept that the values of the therapist are important so that there can be a situation where there is a link between what both therapist and service-user want to achieve. There are, however, many instances when the values of the service-user are opposed to the values of the therapist. This can be exemplified within a school environment in which the pupils do not want to achieve what their teachers perceive as being important. This is supported by research that has been completed on the 'chava' subculture within the north-east of England. It is also acknowledged by Anne Watson (2004) in her discussion of the failings of the 14–19 curriculum within the UK. Watson argues that it is not so much that the curriculum is a bad idea, it is more that there is little awareness of how to unite the values of the pupils and their teachers. This can mean that if a social worker is to attempt using the ideas of Rogers the therapy cannot work because there is no common understanding of what is important and achievable. It is all very well to say that a would/should dilemma should be resolved but a service-user can only be directed to their 'inner beautiful self' if they perceive that self through a shared sense of identity with their therapist. Malim and Birch (1998, p803) develop this criticism by arguing that a critical limitation with humanist therapies relates to the assumption that 'self-actualisation' is a principal human motivation. Self-actualisation may motivate particular groups of individuals but it cannot be assumed to be a universal characteristic of every human being at every point in time.

It may be argued that psychodynamic therapy has as many limitations as uses. The model is not based upon a sound methodology and many of the theoretical ideas can be challenged. It is a theory that is built upon assumptions of how the mind operates. If this is the case, it can be argued that any successes within psychodynamic theory are due to good fortune as much as anything else. A more significant critique of psychodynamic therapy from a social work perspective is that it is a theory that is laden with negative value assumptions. The therapist is perceived to be in control of interpreting the service-user's problems. The classic image of the psychiatric couch can be applied to psychodynamic theory. This means that there is no equality of dialogue. As opposed to influencing the therapeutic process, the service-user is effectively disempowered by a therapist who tells 'what should be done' in order to resolve 'fixated behaviour'. Malim and Birch (1998, p802) reinforce this criticism by emphasising that within psychoanalytical therapies there are problems of 'validation'. It may be suggested that within psychodynamic therapy the truth is invented as opposed to being truth in itself.

The cognitive psychology of Jean Piaget can also be criticised. It is a theory that may have been mistranslated and turned into an unworkable model of the mind. Can it be accepted that the human brain moves through the stages that have become accepted as integral to Piaget's model? If not and if thoughts develop through more of a process than a movement through distinct stages of development it means that the potential application of cognitive therapy is called into question. A further criticism is that although one can take apart a computer and identify the microchips making up its component parts, the human brain is altogether more complex. All sorts of factors that are not necessarily conscious inform cognitive processes. This may mean that a perspective that focuses upon what happens after a stimulus but before a response is dealing with part of the picture, but not the whole picture of human thought. A further criticism of cognitive therapy is that the service-user's problem behaviours or thoughts are always changed to those that the therapist sees as being acceptable. Malim and Birch (1998, p801) question whether it can always be the case that the therapist has the correct perspective on the world and that the service-user's cognitive outlook is in need of total change.

The biological therapies that are available to social work may be criticised because of what we do not know as opposed to what we do know. There is still much work that needs to be done in order to understand the hormonal and genetic composition of the brain. There is also a degree of uncertainty as to why some chemical treatments work with some service-users and yet the same treatments are less effective with other individuals who have the same symptoms. This anxiety can be combined with the concern existing over the side effects of drug-based therapy and the ethical implications this has for service-users. Taking a particular pill might make someone less aggressive but if the consequences are the docility exemplified in *One Flew Over the Cuckoo's Nest* it may be argued that this effectively reduces the individual's life chances. There is also the critique that biological psychology is reductionist. It reduces the complex functioning of the brain to the relationship existing between genes, chromosomes and hormones. By concentrating the focus on this single area it can be argued that there is a possibility that other variables influencing human thought and behaviour are overlooked.

C H A P T E R   S U M M A R Y

In this opening chapter psychology has been likened to an 'academic ship of fools'. It is a complex discipline with competing views on how the subject ought to be studied. It is a diverse discipline with a range of identifiable 'sub-areas' of interest. There are a number of schools of psychology, each of which has adopted its own model of the person. The chapter has defined and elaborated upon five major perspectives that are of use to social workers. Examples of specific therapies that are available to social work have been provided and there has been a critical appraisal of each of the therapies. It may be argued that the best way to apply psychology to social work is to combine the perspectives and their therapies in such a way that the complex needs of individuals are more likely to be met. If this is done, it produces a holistic approach to meeting service-user needs. If these therapies are combined with other perspectives from health and counselling there is the further likelihood that effective service can be delivered to service-users. It may be argued that this is the best way to apply psychology to social work.

Self-assessment questions

1.1 What are the five major schools of psychology?

1.2 How can the schools of psychology be best applied by social workers to help service-users?

1.3 Give an example of a strength and a weakness of each of the psychological schools of thought.

FURTHER READING

Gross, RD (2005) *Psychology: The science of mind and behaviour*, 5th edition, London: Hodder Arnold.

An excellent textbook in terms of depth of content and analysis but the material is not always related to specific social care contexts.

Malim, T and Birch, A (2000) *Introductory psychology*. London: Palgrave Macmillan.

An excellent textbook that is written in an accessible way and makes clear links to applying psychology to social care.

Chapter 2
Psychology and communication

A C H I E V I N G   A   S O C I A L   W O R K   D E G R E E

This chapter will begin to help you to meet the following National Occupational Standards:

Key Role 1: Prepare for and work with individuals, families, carers, groups and communities to assess their needs and circumstances.

- Work with individuals, families, carers, groups and communities to help them make informed decisions.

Key Role 2: Plan, carry out, review and evaluate social work practice with individuals, families, carers, groups, communities and other professionals.

- Interact with individuals, families, carers, groups and communities to achieve change and development and to improve life opportunities.

Key Role 3: Support individuals to represent their needs, views and circumstances.

- Advocate with and on behalf of individuals, families, carers and communities.

Key Role 6: Demonstrate professional competence in social work practice.

- Contribute to the promotion of best social work practice.

It will also introduce you to the following academic standards as set out in the social work subject benchmark statement:

3.1.4 Social work theory

Research-based concepts and critical explanations from social work theory and other disciplines that contribute to the knowledge base of social work including their distinctive epistemological status and application to practice.

The relevance of psychological and physiological perspectives to understanding individual and social development and functioning.

3.1.5 The nature of social work practice

The factors and processes that facilitate effective interdisciplinary, interprofessional and interagency collaboration and partnership.

3.2.2 Problem-solving skills

3.2.3 Communication skills

Listen actively to others, engage appropriately with the life experiences of service-users, understand accurately their viewpoint and overcome personal prejudices to respond appropriately to a range of complex personal and interpersonal situations.

Use both verbal and non-verbal cues to guide interpretation.

Identify and use opportunities for purposeful and supportive communication with service-users within their everyday situations.

3.2.2.3 Analysis and synthesis

Assess the merits of contrasting theories, explanations, research, policies and procedures.

3.2.2.4 Intervention and evaluation

Build and sustain purposeful relationships with people and organisations in community-based and interprofessional contexts including group care.

3.2.3.1 Managing problem-solving activities

Think logically and systematically.

The subject skills highlighted to demonstrate knowledge include:

- Assess human situations, taking into account a variety of factors.
- Assess the merits of contrasting theories, explanations, research, policies and procedures.
- Identify and keep under review your own personal and professional boundaries.

Introduction

Better to remain silent and be thought a fool than to speak out and remove all doubt.
(Abraham Lincloln, 1809–1865)

Abraham Lincoln draws attention to the importance of effective communication within the above quotation. Most people would not like to be thought a 'fool' but there is often a compulsion to feel that we will be thought of as being somehow 'inferior' if we say nothing. It can be argued that this is when communication becomes 'foolish'. It can also be argued that whenever we communicate to appease particular contexts we are not being true to ourselves. This in turn means that whenever we are not true to ourselves we are communicating ineffectively. In other words, knowing how to communicate effectively is essential if the relationship between social worker and service-user is to be characterised by best practice.

This chapter discusses the significance of communication in relation to service-user/social worker interaction. Communication is understood in this context as referring to the act of *exchanging thoughts, messages, and information by speech, signals, writing or behaviour* (www.dictionary.reference.com). The chapter uses the work of Koprowska (2005) in order to explore the importance of effective communication methods for social workers. The chapter will conclude by analysing communication in the light of Eric Berne's transactional analysis. A theme within the chapter is that if social workers and service-users apply the recommendations of Berne's classic theory, interpersonal communication is likely to be characterised by good practice.

Koprowska emphasises the significance of a *goal-directed collaborative working alliance with service-users* so that social workers are *approachable, warm, attentive, respectful, interested and understanding* (2005, p72). This working practice is the ideal of the GSCC. In 2002 the GSCC reiterated the importance of having good communication if there is to be effective social work practice. This recommendation is also supported by the Department of Health as they have included communication as one of the five categories of learning for the social work degree. This aspect of practice is developed throughout the chapter by reflecting on the contribution psychology makes to understanding human communication. The formative activities within the chapter reinforce and develop your learning in relation to the psychology of communication. A central aim of the chapter is to raise your awareness of the impact of communication methods on social work practice.

After reading this chapter you should be able to:

- identify different forms of communication;
- classify communication into categories (interpersonal, verbal, vocal non-verbal, and non-vocal communication);
- identify forms of verbal communication and recognise the skills that promote effective verbal communication;
- identify forms of non-verbal communication and recognise the skills that promote effective non-verbal communication;

- critically appraise how the relationship between social workers and service-users can be enhanced through the application of Eric Berne's transactional analysis.

The importance of communication within the service-user/social worker relationship has been highlighted in a number of well publicised inquiries that have attempted to identify how best practice can be ensured within social work. From the recommendations following the death of Maria Colwell in the 1970s to the main findings of Lord Laming's inquiry into the death of Victoria Climbié, good communication methods within social work would appear to be an essential requirement of effective social work practice. This means that your effectiveness as a social worker can be crucially linked to your awareness of your communications skills and those of the service-users. It means that much effective social work practice is determined by communication skills. As in other aspects of life, professional and otherwise, factors such as tone of voice and body language have a significant impact on the relationship that develops between a social worker and his or her service-users.

Forms of communication

One could argue that humans have unique communication methods within the known world. Malim and Birch (1998) use the work of Noam Chomsky (1972) to support this argument. Chomsky has popularised the difference between human and non-human communication. Whereas mammals such as cats and dogs communicate at a 'surface' level, humans communicate using both 'surface' and 'deep' meanings. To phrase this simply, human communication has depths beyond the surface meaning of verbal and non-verbal communication. Dogs may bark in different ways according to different stimuli but the meaning of the communication is at a 'surface' level. One can tell what the dog means by the sound of the bark and there is no clear 'reading between the lines'. The argument runs that human communication is altogether more complex. As well as the 'surface' meanings denoted by one's tone of voice there are also 'deep' metaphorical meanings. To give an example, the sentence 'light breaks where no sun shines' could mean that it is light even though the sun is not shining or it could also be a metaphor denoting the triumph of life over death. Chomsky argues that human communication is so complex because of the presence within the brain of a 'Language Acquisition Device' (LAD). This cognitive function enables humans to play word games and communicate in many varied complex ways. Koprowska (2005) applies the 'System for Analyzing Verbal Interaction' in her analysis of interpersonal communication. This system is an excellent example of the application of the Language Acquisition Device because it identifies the complex 'deep' meanings of human communication.

There are different forms of communication that influence the relationship between a social worker and his or her service-users. It could be argued that communication methods have become increasingly complex as the human Language Acquisition Device has evolved. We now have new forms of communication such as 'texting', 'e-mail' and mobile phones. These newer forms of communication are used in both positive and negative ways. Both types of communication reveal the complexity and creativity of human communication.

Categories of communication

Table 2.1 summarises the forms of communication that many of us use and are familiar with. All of these forms of communication influence the social work relationship to a significant extent.

Table 2.1 *Categories of communication*

Interpersonal communication	Any communication that takes place between two or more people
Verbal communication	Communication using words and conversation
Non-verbal communication	All interpersonal communication other than spoken communication including textual and other visual forms of communication. Non-verbal communication can also be defined as including communication by vocal sounds
Vocal communication	Aspects of speech associated with vocal sounds in relation to intonation, pitch and pauses of the voice
Non-vocal communication	All non-speech related communication such as eye contact and communicating through appearance

---

ACTIVITY **2.1**

Some social workers have been accused of patronising their service-users if their communication methods reinforce the notion that the service-users are 'dependent' on social workers. Under which of the headings in Table 2.1 would you expect to identify this form of behaviour?

COMMENT

'Patronising' service-users could be classified under all of the table headings.

- Verbal communication. *An example of patronising service-users through verbal communication is talking to the service-user in a way that is condescending. A more specific example would be to assume that an older person always requires help, or addressing a service-user with learning disabilities in 'baby talk'. This unfortunate consequence can be a result of the best of intentions. Many social workers automatically assume that the people they work with require help and this leads them to treat their service-users as if they were vulnerable and childlike.*

- Non-verbal communication. *This can result in patronising service-users by posture and facial expressions. If your posture is over-relaxed it may communicate a message that you do not take your service-user seriously. Likewise if you are always smiling at your service-users it can also suggest that you consider them to be 'childlike' individuals who need to be looked after.*

- Vocal communication. *There may be nothing wrong with the words that you are using to communicate with a service-user but the tone of your voice may be patronising. If every sentence ends with an inflection your tone of voice may sound as if you are talking to a child.*

- Non-vocal communication. *One's gaze often reveals the judgements that are being made about particular service-users. Staring for prolonged periods at a service-user can reinforce a message that the individual is unusual and not capable of independent living.*

The following case study develops these themes in relation to the implications that communication methods can have for effective social practice.

Michael is 16 and he has a number of forms of challenging behaviour that mean that he can be physically aggressive. Michael's social worker (Steven) finds this behaviour very difficult, the communication strategies that are applied to the relationship are especially important. Steven believes in a number of values that may be described as 'old-fashioned'. He thinks that aggressive behaviour is 'bad behaviour'. This means that Steven's verbal and non-verbal communication with Michael can be negative. The other staff who work with Michael are aware of the tension that appears to exist between Steven and Michael. One staff member, Susan, suggested that Steven's way of communicating with Michael actually exacerbates the relationship. It led Susan to conclude that Michael's needs would only be met if he had staff working with him who employed positive communication strategies.

Forms of verbal communication

As stated in Table 2.1, verbal communication refers to communication using words and conversation. Koprowska (2005, p79) argues that *providing information that is clear and context-related underpins social work practice*. As with all forms of communication there are some individuals who communicate effectively and others whose verbal communication skills need to be developed. Underdeveloped verbal skills may be a product of difficulties in relation to a number of important areas that are identified by Koprowska as including *listening; providing information; gathering information; paraphrasing and summarising; using commands and corrective feedback; and bringing relationships to an end* (2005, p72). It can be argued that as a social worker it is particularly important to try to have as highly developed skills as possible within these identified areas if one's verbal communication is to be effective.

Koprowska (2005, p77) identifies listening as being especially important in the process of communication. Listening is regarded as being *an essential part of the turn-taking that characterises human interaction*. Within social work it is deemed as being particularly important to listen. Koprowska continues her argument by saying that listening enhances verbal interaction because when we listen to others we are effectively giving value to what they are saying. This enables a social worker to *hold* the service-user's *story in our mind and theirs'* (2005, p77). This in turn helps in identifying the processes that need to be applied in identifying changes that need to be made.

In order to enhance verbal communication it can be suggested that it is important to provide information that is readily understood. Koprowska (2005, p79) emphasises the significance of providing information that is factual. If our verbal communication is to be of a high standard it is important that we provide facts at a pace that the service-user can manage. It is also important to provide verbal communication about boundaries.

Koprowska (2005, p79) argues that in the 'System for Analyzing Verbal Interaction' providing verbal boundaries is 'green light' behaviour because it is answering inner-person questions. *I am going to be with you for 30 minutes* is an example of verbal communication that provides a positive boundary. A further important way of enhancing verbal communication is to offer appropriate, effective explanations of professional practice. Many service-users know very little about social work other than the impressions they have formed about the profession. It is, therefore, particularly important that the service-users are made aware of what professional processes are going to affect them when it is in their best interests to know about these processes. Koprowska (2005, p80) goes on to emphasise the importance of *opinions and proposals* in determining the effectiveness of communication. It is essential that we let service-users know about our opinions and proposals if the professional relationship is to be congruent. 'Proposals' ought to be thought of as being *possibilities and choices* (2005, p80) that are offered to service-users. In enhancing verbal communication it is also important to ensure that 'opinions' are supported by facts. In other words, we should not verbally communicate that a service-user is 'difficult' if there are no facts to support what is effectively a negative value judgement. Alongside these aspects of good practice, it is imperative that verbal communication communicates empathy. Koprowska (2005) emphasises the importance of using empathic statements such as *I can see that this really has affected you*. Using verbal communication in this way can enhance the professional relationship and lead to best practice.

If we put good verbal skills into effect our gathering of information is likely to be of a high standard. Koprowska (2005) draws attention to three different kinds of questions that may be phrased as narrow questions, broad questions and inner-person questions. Narrow questions are very similar to closed questions as they can be answered using 'yes/no' answers. Broad questions are similar to open questions because they encourage others to give their views and opinions. Inner-person questions are phrased as being both narrow and broad. Their critical characteristic is that they aim to elicit individual feelings and emotions. Questions such as *are you angry with me?* and *how do you feel about living alone?* are examples of inner-person questions. It can be argued that they are especially good for social work practice because they encourage the empathic process. The ideal is to try to develop this type of question at the expense of 'leading questions'. As Koprowska argues, leading questions such as *don't you think it would be a good idea to go to the family centre?* do little other than coerce the other person into agreement (2005, p84). They diminish the quality of verbal communication.

Koprowska (2005, p87) draws attention to the importance of paraphrasing and summarising if verbal communication is to be of a high standard. Paraphrasing can be understood as repeating back to a service-user what they have said. It is an aspect of verbal communication that is considered to be important because it helps to check understanding and maximise interaction. Summarising is equally important because it helps to communicate the individual's shared goals. In meetings with service-users it is important to be aware of the disempowerment they may feel because they do not necessarily 'own the process'. By summarising aims and objectives it becomes easier to lessen this feeling of disempowerment. If these skills of verbal communication can be combined with appropriate commands and corrective feedback, assertive verbal communication can be the central characteristic of the social worker/service-user relationship.

Koprowska (2005, p 89) draws attention to the importance of bringing working relationships to a positive end. It can be argued that if one's verbal skills are good it is easier to provide an assertive conclusion to a working relationship. The ideal is to avoid unplanned endings, especially so that the relationship between the social worker and the service-user does not break down. By considering what needs to be said at the conclusion of a meeting so that the encounter ends on a note of congruence, best practice can be put into effect.

Forms of non-verbal communication

In Table 2.1 non-verbal communication is explained as being interpersonal communication that is not spoken, including textual and other visual forms of communication. It is a form of communication that can also be defined as including communication by vocal sounds. Body language, eye contact, gaze, posture, body position, smell, touch, appearance, tone of voice and facial expressions are all important aspects of non-verbal communication influencing the service-user/social worker relationship. It is important to remember that non-verbal communication is often prompted by conversation. We hear someone's tone of voice and make a facial expression. We hear someone's verbal language and alter our body language accordingly. In other words it can be argued that both non-verbal and non-vocal communication is often critically linked to verbal/vocal stimuli.

Koprowska (2005) has identified the importance of listening in enhancing the relationship between a social worker and a service-user. It can be argued that listening depends upon aspects of non-verbal communication such as gesture and gaze so it is essential that social workers are aware of how to support the listening process through effective non-verbal communication.

Some general guidance as to how to enhance non-verbal communication is possible but it is also important to be aware that interpretations of non-verbal communication vary according to culture. As Knapp and Daly argue, *cultural characteristics serve as identity badges* (2002, p258) in relation to interpersonal communication. In other words what we interpret as appropriate non-verbal communication can be interpreted differently in another culture. Within the context of social work it is important to be aware of body language, body position and posture. Body language that is too open or too closed is unlikely to facilitate a positive professional working relationship. Likewise standing too close to a service-user or keeping too remote a distance can adversely affect the professional relationship. Either appearing to be too relaxed or too formal are both extreme messages that harm the communication of a social worker and his or her service-user. It is also important to have appropriate eye contact. In other words, a social worker should neither 'stare' at a service-user nor avoid all eye contact. Both forms of non-verbal communication are likely to be interpreted negatively. It is important to strike some sort of balance so that the communication that is occurring appears to be as positive as possible.

It can be argued that appearance, smell, touch and facial expressions are other aspects of non-verbal communication for social workers to be aware of. Many service-users requiring social work support may have low self-esteem so if we reinforce this self-image by reacting negatively to a service-user's smell and/or appearance, the professional relationship is likely to be less than ideal. This does not mean that we avoid issues at the expense of being incongruent. It is more that we should use non-verbal communication in an assertive way so that touch and facial expressions contribute to the empathic relationship that rests at the centre of much positive social work practice.

It can be argued that Koprowska's latest work complements the earlier work of Michael Argyle (1988; also Argyle and Colman, 1995). Argyle emphasises the importance of non-verbal communication (NVC) as it is deemed to be a particularly important aspect of human communication. This reinforces the argument that being aware of positive non-verbal communication is especially important for social workers. It means that the expression of interpersonal attitudes and emotions has a particularly important influence on the social worker/service-user relationship. The consequence is that in the context of this professional relationship our attitudes and feelings about the service-user (both positive and negative) are expressed by our NVC. How we look at a service-user and how we respond with our body language is an especially important factor influencing the nature of this relationship. There is therefore a link between establishing a positive rapport with a service-user and the use of effective non-verbal communication.

A second important aspect of non-verbal communication is described by Argyle as being the function of 'self-presentation'. This refers to the image or impression that we want to communicate to others. For example, the way in which we dress can say much about what we value in the world. If we value traditional interpretations of discipline and punctuality we may dress in a particular way in order to communicate this value. Likewise, if we do not value discipline and punctuality we may choose to express this value judgement through the clothes we choose to wear. In a professional context this can have a significant impact upon the extent to which a service-user feels confident in our professional ability and/or is at ease with the professional relationship.

The work of Argyle and Colman (1995) also reinforces Koprowska's point in relation to non-verbal behaviour supporting and/or complementing what is being communicated verbally. Argyle argues that when we are engaged in conversation with another person, our NVC can serve to control the synchronisation of the interaction (for example when it is time for one person to stop talking and another to begin), to provide feedback on what is being said by the speaker and to indicate whether or not the listener is attending to what is being said. If NVC is not used effectively it can mean that interpersonal interaction is affected adversely. This means that NVC is an extremely important facet of the interaction occurring between social workers and service-users. According to Argyle one of the most important roles of NVC is the expression of emotional states. This means that NVC is a particularly important form of communication for social workers because so much social work relies upon responding effectively at an emotional level. Argyle also emphasises the importance of NVC in managing relationships with postural congruence being an indicator of rapport. Awareness of this aspect of communication will have inevitable consequences for the effectiveness or otherwise of the service-user/social worker relationship.

Remember the ABC of effective communication between social workers and service-users, as illustrated in Figure 2.1.

Appropriate verbal content	+	**B**ody language promoting emotional engagement	=	**C**ongruence!

Figure 2.1 *The 'ABC' of effective communication*

ACTIVITY 2.2

In the previous section of the chapter the idea of how gaze, facial expression, body position and posture affect the social worker/practitioner relationship has been introduced. Think about how these aspects of non-verbal communication can influence the social worker/service-user relationship in more detail.

COMMENT

As we have seen all of the above aspects of non-verbal communication can have an important influence on the relationship between a social worker and a service-user. If, for example, you are working with service-users who have mental health needs one has to be extremely aware of how gaze can influence the relationship. Staring at a paranoid service-user is likely to exacerbate feelings of low self-esteem or paranoia. This non-verbal communication can increase the service-user's levels of anxiety and make them think that they are socially unacceptable. If a social worker regulates his or her gaze so that the service-user does not feel threatened it is more likely that a positive professional relationship will develop. This may enable the service-user to feel empowered and capable of adjusting to meet social expectations.

Earlier in the chapter it was mentioned that facial expression is particularly important in sending out signals about how we feel about someone. Within a social work context a facial expression that is either too serious or too flippant will send out negative messages to the service-users. This will in turn influence the professional social work relationship. To develop this point it may be suggested that the best facial expression is one that is relaxed and sincere so that through one's facial expression a message of positive congruent trust is provided. Many of us make judgements about other people based on their facial expressions so it is extremely important for social workers to understand the importance of this element of interaction.

Whereas it may be argued that gaze and facial expressions convey a more definite impression of what we are thinking, body position and posture may be seen as being more subtle forms of communication. We are often less aware of our posture and body position while being more aware of gaze and facial expression. The ideal is for the social worker/service-user relationship to be enhanced as a result of good body position and posture. A closed body position with folded arms may be interpreted as being a sign that we are uncomfortable with our service-users. Likewise, a rigid body posture may give the impression that we are neither relaxed nor at ease with our service-users. Through having an 'open' body position and a relaxed posture the ideal is to create as positive a message as possible. It is especially important that we ensure that we show awareness of positive non-verbal communication as opposed to trying to 'put on an act'. It can be argued that whereas showing awareness of the importance of positive NVC is demonstrating assertiveness, 'putting on an act' and communicating in an insincere way is likely to have as negative a consequence as being unaware of NVC altogether.

Most of us have met people who appear to be 'naturals' in particular contexts. There are academic, teaching, parental, sporting, dancing and social 'naturals'. There are also social work 'naturals' and it can be proposed that this natural quality is always apparent within those individuals who are able to use NVC effectively. An excellent example of the use of positive NVC appears in the ITV drama Lost for Words. One of the support workers working with older service-users is particularly aware of the difficulties that her service-users have with verbal communication. This means that the support worker uses open body language and gestures, positive facial expressions and appropriate eye contact to provide as non-threatening a message as possible to her older service-users. By way of a contrast, the next case study reveals the difficulties that appear within the social work relationship if NVC is not used effectively.

CASE STUDY

Yasmin is 25 and she is extremely paranoid as well as having moderate learning disabilities. Her social worker has not had very much experience of working with service-users who have mental health problems and from the moment Sacha met Yasmin she found it hard not to stare at Yasmin's 'haunted' expression. Sacha was not looking forward to working with Yasmin and after briefly shaking hands with Yasmin she folded her arms and held a rigid posture. Although Sacha found it easy to talk at Yasmin, possibly a result of nerves, her NVC did not communicate a relaxed message. At the end of the first meeting Sacha thought that Yasmin seemed to be very withdrawn. Sacha thought of the saying that 'you never get a second chance to make a good first impression' and that her work with Yasmin would be an enormous challenge.

RESEARCH ACTIVITY

During the course of the next week make notes on the forms of NVC you have used.

COMMENT

We shall discuss and appraise the various channels of NVC and their relevance to social worker/service-user interaction in the next section of this chapter. After you have read the remainder of this chapter refer back to your research notes and compare and contrast your findings with the material in this chapter.

As well as identifying the forms of NVC and their impact on the social worker/service-user relationship, it is important to be aware of the complexity of how NVC is experienced. It is possible to divide NVC into four divisions or classifications. This idea is expressed in Figure 2.2. These divisions are important in that they reflect the different influences that can affect the expression and reception of NVC within a professional context. As with all forms of communication there are complex variables influencing the exact ways in which NVC influences the social worker/service-user relationship. This section of the chapter identifies and analyses some of these variables. Figure 2.2 introduces this idea by illustrating that the NVC expressed by the service-user is likely to affect the NVC of the social worker.

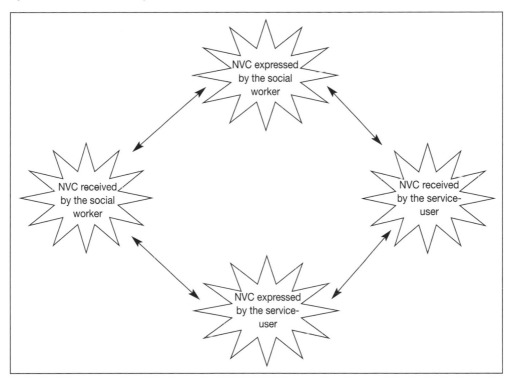

Figure 2.2 *The relationship between expressing and receiving NVC*

Aspects of NVC received by the service-user

The previous case study about Yasmin identifies an example of NVC as experienced by a service-user. The nervous anxiety of an inexperienced social worker exacerbates Yasmin's sense of paranoia. If one's inexperience is expressed by NVC it may evoke feelings of fear and anxiety within service-users. This may in turn add to the difficulties being experienced by the service-user. Generally speaking it can be argued that the service-user is likely to have a heightened sensitivity to NVC, as this is how they will obtain the additional information that they are reluctant to ask about or that they feel the social worker may be intentionally keeping from them. If service-users do have particular needs such as mental health needs, it may also mean that the interpretation of NVC is not accurate and that the interpretation that is given to particular expressions of NVC reinforces negative professional working relationships.

Aspects of NVC expressed by the service-user

The previous case study gives an example of how NVC reinforces negative feelings. Although it is important not to make too many general assumptions about how NVC affects service-users it can be argued that particular service-users can experience a heightened emotional sensitivity that can be expressed through non-verbal channels. Children may be particularly aware of forms of NVC such as facial expressions when they have limited verbal skills. Similarly, NVC may be the social worker's only means of identifying symptoms or problems that the service-user may be unwilling or unable to disclose verbally.

Aspects of NVC received by the social worker

It is important that the social worker receives and correctly interprets the NVC of their service-users. Individuals vary in their level of sensitivity to NVC, but accurate perception is important in interaction as service-users may attempt to control obvious channels but 'leak' this information through less obvious channels. As an example, the service-user may control their state of mind vocally while 'giving the game away' by their gaze.

Aspects of NVC expressed by the social worker

Non-verbal 'signals' transmitted by the social worker can have important implications for the professional relationship. Service-users are likely to benefit significantly from a positive expectation of the professional relationship conveyed by the social worker both verbally and non-verbally. This contributes to the concept of the self-fulfilling prophecy that has been popularised by psychologists such as Albert Bandura (1977). To paraphrase Rogers, it is especially important that we are able to provide congruence so that the relationship between the social worker and his or her service-users is perceived to be as genuine as possible. It can be argued that the perception of such congruence is likely to be enhanced whenever NVC is used effectively.

ACTIVITY 2.3

In the earlier research activity you were asked to observe NVC both in yourself and in other people. This activity requires you to think about the importance of being sensitive to other people's NVC. In completing the activity think about how you feel if other people are insensitive to your NVC. Make a note of situations when you feel that NVC has either been unnoticed or misinterpreted by yourself, a colleague or a service-user. What effect, if any, did this 'breakdown in communication' have on the interaction as a whole?

COMMENT

Although your own reflections will be unique in relation to your own experience it is possible to give some general reflections on how insensitivity to NVC impacts upon the professional relationship between a social worker and his or her service-users. An immediate point that can be made is that if others are insensitive to NVC, tension can become a significant characteristic of the interaction that is taking place. If you are aware of the importance of NVC and do all you can to enhance the communication within the relationship yet someone else disregards your own efforts at providing positive NVC the interpersonal communication within the relationship is likely to deteriorate. These feelings can be based on intuitive judgements. It is easier to know when someone is listening to you or not giving you their full attention. Assessing whether someone is aware of your NVC can be rather more complex. Within this area of uncertainty it may be that you wonder whether a particular service-user dislikes you. This thought may occur within your mind as a result of the responses that are being given to your NVC. Many of us have probably experienced what it feels like to be with someone who looks at their watch every time we speak. The typical interpretation that is given to this type of behaviour is that our views are not being valued. This has an inevitable impact upon the subsequent interaction that is likely to take place.

ACTIVITY **2.4**

Your previous activities in this section of the chapter have focused on NVC in general, that is becoming aware of its existence and its effects on interaction, especially in relation to the issue of sensitivity in identifying NVC. In this activity you will be concerned more specifically with the effects that good and bad NVC have on the quality of social worker/service-user interaction.

Reflect on your experience of social care settings and observe four interactions taking place between colleagues and service-users. Make a note of the quality of NVC that you think is being expressed by both the colleague and the service-user and suggest how this could be improved in order to enhance the interaction.

COMMENT

I remember starting work as a residential social worker in London. My first day at work began at 2 p.m. on a Tuesday afternoon. I was working with two service-users who had paranoid schizophrenia. I was also working with a supervisor I had never met before. It was my first day at work so I wanted to make as good an impression as possible. In general the staff worked from either 7 a.m.–3 p.m. or 2–10 p.m. I remember meeting one of the staff who was leaving work as I was beginning and I told him which service-users I was going to be working with. He wished me 'good luck' in a way that worried me because he seemed to imply that I would have a challenging introduction to residential care. The service-users were out at a day centre and they returned at 3 p.m. Everything seemed OK at first. My supervisor was very experienced but said to me that if things began to get 'out of hand' there was a panic button at the top of the stairs. This unsettled me and when I was intro-duced to one of the service-users called Anthony, I stared at him and gazed into his eyes. I could do nothing other than stand and stare in an awkward fashion. The two service-users had a cup of tea and then suddenly one of them had a very aggressive outburst seizing my supervisor by the hair. I didn't know what to do and froze. My supervisor told me to sound the alarm button. In a few seconds two of the other staff intervened and I was sent down-stairs to work with the 'less demanding' service-users.

When I got home that night I couldn't sleep for worry about what it was going to be like working in the care setting. I also thought about my NVC. I had been a combination of nerves and eagerness to please. I don't think I'd sat down all afternoon and I wondered if this was one of the reasons why the service-user had been so unsettled. Had I been more relaxed and at ease so that my NVC conveyed a relaxed message to the other staff and service-users the whole incident might have been avoided. In future I made sure that I didn't stare at the service-users. I also became more aware of my body language and pos-ture. I was physically bigger than any of the other people in the care setting so I made sure that I sat down as opposed to towering above everyone else. After this beginning things did improve.

Then again ... they couldn't have been any worse than this first encounter!

Interpreting communication with Eric Berne's transactional analysis

Transactional analysis was developed by the Canadian psychologist Eric Berne (1910–70). It can be argued that it has made an influential and interesting contribution to understanding human communication. The advantage of Berne's theory is that it is accessible and it can be used to interpret the quality of communication occurring between individuals and groups.

Berne's transactional analysis proposes that all individuals have three components to their personality. Berne uses the phrase 'ego states' to explain these components. According to the theory there are 'parent', 'adult' and 'child' states. The 'parent state' represents authoritarian characteristics of personality. The 'adult state' represents appropriate interac-tion. The 'child state' represents interaction that is characterised by emotional impulses. Berne argues that all of these categories are present in adults and children. They govern our interpersonal communication.

The theory proposes that when people communicate, they do so according to parent, child or adult states. Figure 2.3 illustrates what Berne means. 'P', 'A' and 'C' refer to parent, adult and child ego states.

Figure 2.3 *Example of a complementary transaction*

In the transaction in Figure 2.3, an appropriate 'adult' question is asked: *How do you feel today?* Likewise an appropriate adult response is given: *I feel fine!* Berne would describe this transaction as 'adult to adult' appropriate interaction. The argument runs that if all of our transactions are characterised by appropriate 'adult to adult' interaction our communication will be high quality.

Berne recognises that many transactions between individuals and groups are not characterised by positive communication methods. There are what are referred to as 'crossed transactions'. This type of communication is illustrated in Figure 2.4.

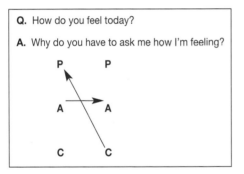

Figure 2.4 *Example of a crossed transaction*

In this transaction an appropriate 'adult' question has been asked but the response is emotional and impulsive as if the respondent is a child retorting to a parent. According to Berne these crossed transactions produce anxiety and stress. There may be any combination of transactions. A 'bossy' authoritarian question such as *Why don't you pull yourself together?* (parent to child) could be answered with *I don't need you to tell me what to do!* (also parent to child). The central point in Berne's argument is that we have to analyse our communication and make our transactions 'adult to adult' if we are to maximise our skills of interpersonal interaction. Within social work, when many encounters with service-users can be characterised with emotion, it is important to ensure as much as possible that our communication is appropriate. It may not always be possible to have 'adult-to-adult' transactions within social work interaction. There may be occasions when an especially insecure service-user is only capable of responding to a 'parent-to-child' encounter. It can also be argued that there are a number of social work service-users who are never capable of having 'adult-to-adult' interaction because of the extent of their mental health needs. Nonetheless, it is important to recognise that we need to analyse our interaction and identify whenever it is possible to communicate with complementary transactions.

Berne has drawn attention to the psychological games that some people choose to play. He describes these encounters as 'ulterior transactions'. This type of communication is illustrated in Figure 2.5.

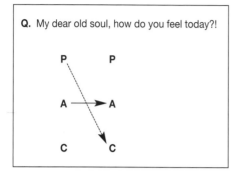

Figure 2.5 *Example of an ulterior transaction*

Ulterior transactions may appear to be 'adult to adult' but they really represent something else. The question *My dear old soul how do you feel today?!* may appear to be 'adult to adult' when in reality the person asking the question wants to be a nurturing parent.

ACTIVITY **2.5**

When you are next at university or at work try to identify examples of the following transactions:

- *adult to adult;*
- *parent to child;*
- *child to parent;*
- *ulterior transactions.*

Write down a short description of each type of transaction and then consider the potential impact on interpersonal interaction.

C H A P T E R   S U M M A R Y

This chapter has discussed some of the psychological interest in communication methods in relation to verbal and non-verbal communication. It can be suggested that NVC serves to communicate interpersonal attitudes and emotions in order to present an image of ourselves to others as a supplement to our verbal communication. The ways in which both verbal and non-verbal communication is relayed to service-users through the social work relationship is likely to either enhance or diminish the effectiveness of this relationship accordingly.

The channels through which NVC is transmitted include gaze and eye contact, facial expression, body language, awareness of personal space, self-presentation and paralanguage. These forms of communication combine with verbal communication in order to present our personality to others. It can be argued that the perception that others have of us depends in part upon how we present and regulate our personality through verbal and NVC.

The channels of NVC play a significant role in the social worker/service-user relationship. It may be argued that the effectiveness of the professional relationship can be 'won or lost' on the basis of the social worker's ability to transmit and interpret appropriate non-verbal signals. This means that being aware of one's communication methods becomes an essential aspect of being an effective social worker. By applying Eric Berne's transactional analysis so that communication is characterised by 'complementary transactions' the ideals of both the GSCC and the Department of Health will hopefully be achieved.

Self-Assessment Questions

2.1 What is:
   – interpersonal communication?
   – vocal behaviour?
   – non-vocal behaviour?

   Give an example of vocal and non-vocal behaviour.

2.2 What are the main channels of NVC?

2.3 What are three types of transaction popularised by Eric Berne?

FURTHER READING

Argyle, M and Colman, AM (eds) (1995) *Social psychology*. London: Longman.

In particular pay attention to Chapter 5 as there is excellent supplementary information on NVC.

Argyle, M (1988) *Bodily communication*. London: Methuen.
An older text but one that is central to the psychology of communication.

Koprowska, J (2005) *Communication and interpersonal skills in social work*. Exeter: Learning Matters.
A current text that contains essential practical information for social workers.

Malim, T and Birch, A (2000) *Introductory psychology*. London: Palgrave Macmillan.
Look for the sections within the book dealing with interpersonal communication.

Chapter 3
Attitudes and beliefs

A C H I E V I N G   A   S O C I A L   W O R K   D E G R E E

This chapter will begin to help you to meet the following National Occupational Standards:

Key Role 1: Prepare for and work with individuals, families, carers, groups and communities to assess their needs and circumstances.

• Prepare for social work contact and involvement.
• Work with individuals, families, carers, groups and communities to help them make informed decisions.

Key Role 2: Plan, carry out, review and evaluate social work practice with individuals, families, carers, groups, communities and other professionals.

• Interact with individuals, families, carers, groups and communities to achieve change and development and to improve life opportunities.
• Work with groups to promote individual growth, development and independence.
• Address behaviour which represents a risk to individuals, families, carers, groups and communities.

Key Role 3: Support individuals to represent their needs, views and circumstances.

• Advocate with and on behalf of individuals, families, carers and communities.

Key Role 5: Manage and be accountable, with supervision and support, for your own social work practice within your own organisation.

• Work with multidisciplinary and multi-organisational teams, networks and systems.

Key Role 6: Demonstrate professional competence in social work practice.

• Work within agreed standards of social work practice and ensure own professional development.
• Contribute to the promotion of best social work practice.

It will also introduce you to the following academic standards as set out in the social work subject benchmark statement:

3.1.1 Social work services and service-users

The social processes (associated with, for example, poverty, unemployment, poor health, disablement, lack of education and other sources of disadvantage) that lead to marginalisation, isolation and exclusion and their impact on the demand for social work services.

3.1.4 Social work theory

Research-based concepts and critical explanations from social work theory and other disciplines that contribute to the knowledge base of social work including their distinctive epistemological status and application to practice.

The relevance of psychological and physiological perspectives to understanding individual and social development and functioning.

3.1.5 The nature of social work practice

The factors and processes that facilitate effective interdisciplinary, interprofessional and interagency collaboration and partnership.

The subject skills highlighted to demonstrate knowledge include:

3.2.2 Problem-solving skills

3.2.2.3 Analysis and synthesis

• Assess the merits of contrasting theories, explanations, research, policies and procedures.
• Analyse and take account of the impact of inequality and discrimination in work with people in particular contexts and problem situations.

Introduction

This chapter discusses the contribution that psychology has made to understanding how attitudes and beliefs are formed. The chapter highlights the complexity of attitude formation and the relationship that exists between attitudes and behaviour. An important theme within the chapter is the importance of being aware of how and when attitudes influence interaction between social workers and service-users. Within the chapter attention is given to the formation of stereotypical attitudes. There is exploration of the relationship that exists between forming stereotypes and having a negative perception of others.

The main aims of the chapter are to:

- identify what attitudes are and how they can be measured;
- identify how attitudes influence behaviour;
- recognise that beliefs about 'well-being' can influence and/or determine behaviour;
- recognise what a stereotype is;
- identify psychological explanations of stereotypical attitudes;
- analyse an example of stereotyping in our society that is relevant to social work practice.

These six aims form the main sections of the chapter.

ACTIVITY **3.1**

Answer each of the following questions:

- *Choose a whole number between 1 and 10.*
- *Double the number.*
- *Add 8.*
- *Halve the number.*
- *Subtract the original number from the new number.*
- *Give the number a letter: 'A' for 1, 'B' for 2, 'C' for 3, 'D' for 4, 'E' for 5, etc.*
- *Think of a European country that begins with the letter.*
- *Think of an animal you might see in a circus that begins with the second letter of the European country!*

Were your last two thoughts:

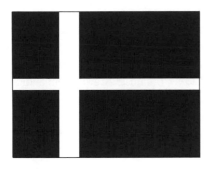

Denmark?

Elephant?

COMMENT

If you have answered the questions accurately there is every possibility that you have thought of 'Denmark' and 'elephant'. If we were to apply the ideas of Howard Gardner (1985) it could be argued that your answer may have been determined by your mathematical intelligence. Your mind will have processed the questions in a particular way. You will then have made sense of the questions so that you are left thinking about 'Danish elephants'. If this has happened you might also be quite curious and amused as to how the thought process has worked. It may even seem 'like magic'!

If you are told that this activity is a simple number trick and that whatever whole number you select between 1 and 10 will always give you a letter 'D' (once you follow the instructions) your attitude towards the activity changes. It is not magic – it is a number trick! It could be argued that the activity says a lot about attitude formation. Once something that seems a bit magical is explained our attitude changes. Something that seems novel and unusual becomes old and ordinary. Reflect on how your attitude to the activity is changing and why it is changing if indeed it is changing. Much of what you are now thinking interests psychologists about attitude formation. Key questions include why we have initial attitudes and how these attitudes develop and influence subsequent behaviour. This chapter deals with both of these themes.

What are attitudes and how can they be measured?

The term 'attitude' has been defined in a variety of ways in formal psychological studies. A definition that has been popularised is that *an attitude is a mental and neural state of readiness organised through experience, exerting a directive and dynamic influence upon the individual's response to all objects and situations with which it is related* (Allport, 1935, p810). Put simply, this means that attitudes are states of mind that affect behaviour and appearance. It may be suggested that this definition has had a significant influence on the understanding of what is meant by the word 'attitudes'.

ACTIVITY 3.2

Think about the Allport definition of 'attitudes' and then write out what you understand by the term.

COMMENT

Attitudes are often equated with views or opinions about particular issues. In our society having an attitude is not always considered to be something positive. The phrase 'having attitude' can mean that a particular person is difficult to deal with. The image that many people may have of particular groups of society is that they have an 'attitude problem'. This means that attitudes can be said to correspond to the Allport definition. Attitudes are mental states affecting behaviour and appearance.

McGuire (1989) develops the Allport understanding of attitudes by drawing attention to the factors influencing attitude formation. According to McGuire, an attitude has three components. There are cognitive mental processes, affective emotions and behavioural components. In other words, an attitude is a thought in the mind that is influenced by emotions and behavioural experiences. This point can be exemplified by analysing any attitude we may have. If we have a favourable attitude towards a person the argument runs that this thought is present within the mind because of the interplay between emotional responses and behavioural experiences. We like the person because we have had positive behavioural interaction with them and this influences our emotional response towards the individual. This in turn produces a positive thought in our mind. This point can be developed in relation to CBT (or cognitive behavioural therapy). It may be possible to influence cognitive thoughts by associating particular phenomena with 'positive' or 'negative' experiences. This therapy has been discussed in Chapter 1. We argued that a difficulty with cognitive-behavioural therapy is that explanations about behaviour are offered using models of cognitive processes that are theoretical as opposed to being 'reality'. We cannot actually observe the human brain forming attitudes in response to emotions and behavioural experiences. We can only assume that this is the case. If we use the words of Clifford Geertz (1988), it means that the argument becomes rather like *the lady sawed in half*, that is *done* but *never really done at all*.

What can be said is that attitude formation is a complex process reliant upon a number of intellectual, emotional and experiential factors. Ajzen (1988) reinforces this point by identifying that we do not always behave in a way that is consistent with our attitudes. Even when we have formed an attitude the extent to which that attitude determines behaviour varies from individual to individual.

It can be argued that attitudes represent responses to people but that these responses to people do not necessarily mean that we are able to predict behaviour. La Piere (1934) popularised this argument. He conducted a research project in which he travelled across America with two Chinese friends staying in 66 hotels and visiting 184 restaurants. During this time La Piere was only refused service once. He then sent a questionnaire to the organisations he had visited and 92 per cent said that they would not accept Chinese customers! This reinforces the point that attitudes do not predict overt behaviour. When you completed Activity 3.1 you would have formed some sort of attitude but this would not have necessarily determined your immediate behaviour. Ajzen (1989) developed these themes to argue that conscious behavioural control is a defining feature in determining behaviour. Fazio (1986) supported this idea by drawing attention to the importance of strength of attitude in that this will strongly influence behavioural control. An example might be that although we want to work in a professional manner we form an emotional attachment with a particular service-user. This may mean that we devote enormous amounts of time and energy to one individual as opposed to using our time for the benefit of all our service-users.

Zajonc (1968) made a further contribution to understanding attitude formation by arguing that repeated exposure to phenomena influence attitudes. The phrase 'better the devil you know' summarises this idea. The unfamiliar and the new may be perceived as a threat and our attitude is therefore less favourable. An example is seen with media personalities on television all the time. Some people enjoy a familiar face and feel comfortable with the same circumstances. There are of course other individuals who experience that their attitudes are affected by opposing factors, as they prefer what is not familiar! The general conclusion that can be made in this section of the chapter is that attitude formation is influenced by highly complex variables.

Measuring attitudes

Just as there are different understandings of what attitudes are so there are different ideas about how one can and should measure attitudes. One might measure attitudes statistically. A common technique is to use 'closed' questions in a questionnaire and then present a statistical breakdown of who has answered 'yes' and who has answered 'no' to particular questions. Another technique is to include 'open' questions in a questionnaire that cannot be answered 'yes' or 'no'. The aim of these questions is to gather the detailed views of the interviewees. A further method uses what are referred to as the 'Likert scale' or 'Q Sort Repertory' questions. These questions typically give a respondent a statement to think about. They then ask if the respondent 'strongly agrees, agrees, disagrees, strongly disagrees' with the statement. A further example follows:

What is your attitude to 'continuing social work professional training'?

    (a)   *A luxury*

    (b)   *An investment*

    (c)   *A necessity*

    (d)   *None of these*

'Likert scale' or 'Q Sort Repertory' questions are linked to some of the fundamental ideas in humanist psychology. Within humanism it is accepted that all individuals think in a unique way. This means that individual attitudes are likely to be many and varied so the questions that measure attitudes need to take this principle into consideration. Questions are designed to facilitate individual consideration of issues so that the responses being given are neither uniform nor unilateral. Another example of a 'Q Sort question' that could be applied to social work is:

> *Which of the following responses summarises your attitude to the idea that social workers do more good than harm to society?*
>
> > *Strongly agree*
> >
> > *Agree*
> >
> > *Disagree*
> >
> > *Strongly disagree*

ACTIVITY 3.3

Imagine the following scenario. You have been asked to research into 'contemporary attitudes towards services for older people in the UK' and you have constructed a questionnaire that you think measures these attitudes. You have administered this questionnaire to 50 people and your results show that a high proportion of the people in your study view 'services for older people' in a negative way. As a trainee social worker you have read Mithran Samuel's (2006) article about the ineffective nature of 'services for older people'. How could a publicity campaign to raise awareness of the need to change attitudes to services for older people be put into action? Make a note of the points you would want to see included in the campaign and of how you would go about turning these points into a persuasive message.

How attitudes influence behaviour

It can be suggested that if you know a person's attitude towards X (either an object or a behaviour), you should be able to predict their behaviour. As a simple example, if someone views social work in a negative way it can be predicted that they are unlikely to work with social workers in a positive way. It can also be assumed that if this attitude is changed from being negative to positive the working relationship with the social worker will improve. However, it is important to emphasise that the relationship between attitudes and behaviour is not that simple. Fishbein and Ajzen (1975) developed this idea in their algebraic representation of the relationship between attitudes and behaviour. Their 'Theory of Reasoned Action' proposes that:

Attitude (A) + Subjective Norm (SN) = Behavioural Intention (BI)

In this equation, Fishbein and Ajzen understand 'attitude' as being a combination of beliefs about the consequences of a particular form of behaviour alongside the individual's evaluation of these consequences. 'Subjective norm' is composed of beliefs about what other people think the individual should do alongside the motivation to comply with this belief. This means that if we can obtain measures, or values, for 'A' and for 'SN' we can then predict whether or not the individual intends to perform the behaviour in question.

This points to the importance of how 'values' influence behaviour. To give an example, if you value the importance of study because it will help you to get a good social work degree and you are highly motivated to achieve this ambition you are more likely to be a diligent student. In this example this is because you have a positive attitude towards becoming a social worker. If your family and friends also believe that your ambition to be a social worker is good and you value their opinion, your behaviour is even more likely to conform to being a diligent student. In other words your subjective norm is reinforcing your attitude. According to the model the more attitude and subjective norm reinforce each other the more likely it is to predict particular forms of behaviour. Likewise if your attitude is adversely affected by your subjective norm, your behavioural intention may not be the same as your attitude. If you have been raised as a Catholic and you leave home to go to university with peers who are not Catholics, their influence may mean that you are less likely to behave in a way that is consistent with your Catholic attitudes. In this example the expression of your individual attitude has been altered by your subjective norm.

The Fishbein and Ajzen model has been used to predict behavioural intentions in a number of areas, such as dental care and contraceptive use. According to Pennington et al. (2002) the model is based on the assumption that if we know what a person's beliefs are in relation to a specific type of behaviour, and we know how they perceive social pressures in relation to performing that behaviour, we should then be able to predict whether or not they will actually carry out that behaviour. Although this particular model for predicting behavioural intention has not been specifically designed to be applied in the field of social care it is perfectly appropriate to apply it in order to help us to understand social worker and service-user behaviour.

It can be argued that Fishbein and Ajzen's formula is particularly relevant for assessing the likelihood of whether behavioural therapies such as token economy are likely to work. In Chapter 1 we identified that the model is less likely to be effective in situations where the service-users do not share the same values as those who are implementing the programme. If a service-user's peer group have alternative values to those implementing the programme there is every likelihood that the behavioural intention to follow the programme will be lessened. This may mean that it is possible to predict that token economy programmes are only likely to produce effective results with service-users whose attitudes are reinforced by peers who share the same values as the person implementing the programme. This would mean that four-year-old children in a primary school setting sharing similar values to their teachers are more likely to follow a token economy programme than adolescents whose values are at odds with their teachers.

How beliefs about health and well-being influence behaviour

Rosenstock's (1966) 'Health Belief Model' explores individual beliefs about health and illness and their impact on the practising of health behaviours. According to the model two main factors influence an individual's health beliefs. These components are the degree to which a person perceives a personal threat to their health and the perception that particular health behaviours will be effective in reducing that threat.

Stainton-Rogers (1991) developed Rosenstock's work to move away from studying the 'professional' views and opinions as provided by health professionals towards a consideration of 'lay' beliefs about the causes and consequences of health and illness. This development reflects the recognition of the importance of the beliefs that the individual holds in relation to health and illness. It means that an individual's perception of the cause of their own well-being influences their perception of the appropriateness of the practitioner's advice and treatment, and ultimately their willingness to comply with that treatment. If we apply this idea to social work it can be argued that shared values between service-users and social workers become extremely important within the service-user/social worker relationship. The perception of what makes an individual socially effective becomes a critical factor in complying with the recommendations of a social worker.

Chapter 1 summarised the main ideas of Carl Rogers' client-centred therapy. It can be argued that an unanswered question within the Rogerian model is: *What happens if a service-user does not share the same values as the social worker?* According to the health belief model the consequences are likely to mean that the individual will not comply with the recommendations of the social worker.

This means that we have to become especially aware of how we communicate with our service-users. Chapter 2 of the book has drawn attention to the importance of verbal and non-verbal communication within social work practice. Rosenstock's (1966) health belief model implies that it is particularly important for social workers to ensure that their service-users have a favourable attitude to social work. For social work practice to be effective it is vital that a service-user shares the social worker's evaluation of what is likely to threaten well-being and what behaviour must be adopted if this threat is to be reduced.

RESEARCH ACTIVITY

Over the next week or so, talk to family, friends, service-users and colleagues about what they see as being the causes of social well-being. What affects whether they are socially successful? Analyse whether these attitudes equate with some of the core social work values. Assess whether or not different people hold the same or similar beliefs, or if there is a wide diversity between the various people you have talked to.

What is a stereotype?

This section of the chapter discusses psychological contributions to understanding stereotyping and prejudice.

ACTIVITY **3.4**

Write out a definition of what you understand by the word stereotype.

COMMENT

The Collins English Dictionary defines a stereotype as an image or conception that is shared by all members of a social group.

Lippman (1922) popularised the phrase 'stereotype' and explained the term by describing it as referring to the 'pictures in our heads' we have of other people. Lippman viewed stereotypes as being a means whereby people protect their relative standing in society. Deaux and Lewis (1983) used this understanding of stereotype in relation to western attitudes about men and women. Whereas men are considered to be 'independent and competitive' women are seen as being 'warm and emotional'. Linssen and Hagendoorn (1994) have developed this work in relation to European students' stereotypical images of northern and southern European national characteristics. Whereas northern nations have been perceived as being 'efficient' southern Europeans are identified as being 'characterised by emotion'.

Stereotyping in itself is not necessarily negative. It is something that all of us engage in to form our views of the world. Nevertheless, it may also be argued that stereotyping is the cause of many prejudicial attitudes. At the centre of the prejudicial attitude is the process of labelling negative attributes to particular individuals. It can also be argued that much discrimination is based on stereotyping. Discrimination is understood in this context as referring to putting prejudicial attitudes into effect. Skelt proposes that *being seen as different can lead to discrimination and in turn to prejudice* (1993, p70). In other words there is a palpable link between prejudice and discrimination. Although discrimination may be a 'neutral' term it is important that unfair, prejudicial and negative forms of discrimination are prevented if good social practice is to occur.

It can be argued that a number of sections of our society experience prejudice and discrimination. The expression of these attitudes may be overt but it may also be subtle so that it changes with the ways in which forms of social expression evolve. Prejudice and discrimination may always have been a part of society but today it is found on the Internet and in text messages, an old social evil transformed into a new virulent strain. As Chapter 2 has explained, human communication methods are many and varied. The communication of prejudicial attitudes is just as diverse and varied. The next section of the chapter develops the theoretical basis of this area of social psychology.

ACTIVITY 3.5

If you were asked to explain why prejudice occurs what would you say?

COMMENT

You might say that that prejudice is something inside the individual, perhaps an inborn personality trait that eventually manifests itself later in life and causes the person to hold discriminating attitudes towards certain groups in society. Alternatively you might think that prejudice arises against other people when we realise that they hold different, contradictory views to our own. In this case, prejudice would not be part of our personality but would be seen as a consequence of this realisation of difference between yourself and others. You might also think that prejudice and conflict are the inevitable result of our being part of a particular social group. For example, if you consider yourself to be a socialist you would automatically experience prejudicial views towards those who identify themselves as leaning towards the political right wing.

Malim and Birch (1998) applied the ideas of Albert Bandura (1977) in accounting for the formation and expression of prejudicial attitudes. Bandura has popularised the idea that behaviour is imitated or 'modelled' if there exists a strong emotional attachment to the person exhibiting the behaviour. If this is the case it is possible to predict that prejudicial attitudes will be reinforced within social groups who have a strong emotional bond. This theory can be used within social work to account for some of the recent racist killings within the UK such as the murder of Christopher Alaneme in April 2006. It can be argued that racism is a form of learned behaviour that is likely to be copied when individuals share close emotional bonds with other peers who put their prejudicial actions into effect. The argument can also be exemplified upon considering why there exist prejudicial attitudes towards social workers. There are people who learn to be prejudicial towards social workers even when they have never experienced social work practice. This may be because the individuals are reinforcing attitudes that they have learned from other emotionally influential people.

Psychological explanations of stereotypical attitudes

The comment on Activity 3.5 offers three possible reasons why prejudice has arisen. These explanations are what Pennington et al. (2002) refer to as 'individual', 'interpersonal' and 'intergroup' approaches to the study of prejudice. This links to Thompson's (1997) idea of 'oppression' operating at personal, cultural and structural levels. If we think of our earlier example when we were considering negative attitudes to social work it may be that these attitudes are a complex product of all three factors. This implies that it is a particular individual's personality that inclines him or her to be prejudicial. This predisposition may be reinforced by one's dealings with other individuals at the one-to-one level, the group level and the societal level. It means that the formation of stereotypes can be a complex process that is a combination of individual, interpersonal and social factors.

Person, role and script schemata

Abelson (1981) applies the ideas of cognitive psychology in explaining the formation of prejudicial views. This argument develops the idea that schemata inform human judgements. The argument runs that we may 'pigeonhole' others in relation to three factors. We make judgements about personal characteristics, social roles and social settings. This cognitive approach to understanding stereotyping identifies person, role and script schemata as being particularly important. 'Person schemata' can be explained as being the impressions we form of a particular person's physical characteristics. We may generate a stereotypical attitude of someone because of the way that they look or sound. 'Role schemata' may be understood as being the impressions we form of someone because of their role. If one is introduced to others as a 'social worker' particular emotions may be generated because of this role. 'Script schemata' can be explained as the individual's expectations of what will happen in a particular social situation. Malim and Birch (1998, p576) exemplify this form of schemata by saying that being invited to Buckingham Palace for tea with the Queen will lead to an individual anticipating what is likely to happen in this particular social context. These factors all influence the formation of prejudicial attitudes.

Prototypes, exemplars and stereotypes

Berry (1990) suggests that physical features such as posture, height, weight and facial expressions are particularly important in forming an immediate perception of the person. This perception is then reinforced by a number of other factors. There are 'prototypes' that can be explained as being a vague set of images attached to a particular group of people belonging to a particular category. A prototype is what immediately comes to mind when you think of a group of people. There are 'exemplars' that develop as one becomes more familiar with a group of people and the prototypical representation is changed to a clearer set of assumptions. Berry argues that if individual prototypes are generally shared, they will evolve into exemplars and then become social stereotypes.

Situational emphasis

Zimbardo's (1979) work popularised the idea that prejudicial views can be generated by social situations. Zimbardo reported how Jane Elliott's 'blue eye/brown eye' experiment revealed how discriminatory views can be accepted and put into effect if influential individuals dominate particular social contexts. Elliott conducted the experiment on a class of school children in Iowa by announcing to the class that children with blue eyes were brighter and superior to those with brown eyes. Blue-eyed children were told that they were going to get special privileges such as longer time at break. After one hour of the experiment the effects began to be seen as the work of the brown-eyed children deteriorated. This means that prejudice can be a product of the interpersonal atmosphere of social interaction.

The authoritarian personality

Adorno et al.'s (1950) description of the authoritarian personality applies psychodynamic theory in explaining the formation of prejudicial attitudes. Adorno popularised the notion of a personality type that is 'authoritarian' or intolerant of others. The theory proposed that the personality type has its origins in childhood. It is generated in response to 'strict' parental upbringing. Adorno argued that such a social environment encouraged a 'love/hate' relationship between children and parents. The child 'loves' the parents because they give clear messages of right and wrong, making the child feel secure and aware of boundaries. Conversely the child 'hates' its parents because of the strict physical and emotional punishments that are given. This contradiction produces anxiety and anger that is unconsciously repressed. In later life this unconscious repression is displaced on those who are perceived as being 'weak' and 'inferior'.

Covariation theory

Kelley (1973; Kelley and Thibaut, 1978) explains the formation of prejudicial attitudes by applying what has become popularised as 'covariation theory'. The argument begins by proposing that behaviour is interpreted as being a consequence of either internal (dispositional) causes or external (environmental) causes according to the principle of covariance. When an action and a cause 'covary' or occur together repeatedly, judgements are made about that person. Kelley suggests that judgements are made according to three principles. These judgements are referred to as 'consistency', 'distinctiveness', and 'consensus'.

- Consistency refers to whether the behaviour happens regularly.
- Distinctiveness refers to whether the behaviour is reinforced by similar behaviour elsewhere.
- Consensus refers to whether many or few people exhibit this behaviour.

When a drug addict is blamed for their behaviour and experiences prejudice and discrimination:
- *The behaviour is highly consistent – it happens regularly.*
- *The behaviour has low distinctiveness – the behaviour is associated with other problem behaviour.*
- *It has low consensus – the majority of the population are not addicted to drugs.*

According to Kelley, whenever there is high consistency, low consensus and low distinctiveness the individual is likely to be perceived as being the cause of the behaviour. This may mean that the individual is more likely to experience prejudice and discrimination. This is because, as the cause of the behaviour is attributed to the individual, there may be a less than sympathetic response from those who are judging the behaviour. In contrast to accepting that environmental factors are the cause of the behaviour, the individual is seen as being at fault.

When someone takes drugs and the blame is not directed towards them:

- *The behaviour has low consistency – it is highly exceptional behaviour that is inconsistent with how the individual usually behaves.*
- *The behaviour is highly distinctive – this is the first 'risky' example of behaviour that has ever been noticed from someone who usually appears to behave in a 'normal' way.*
- *The behaviour has high consensus – increasing numbers of people in society are perceived as taking casual drugs.*

ACTIVITY 3.6

What behavioural expectations might you have of:

- *an authoritarian service-user?*
- *an authoritarian social worker?*

How do you think the following combinations would affect the service-user/social worker relationship?

- *An authoritarian service-user with a non-authoritarian social worker*
- *A non-authoritarian service-user with an authoritarian social worker*
- *An authoritarian service-user with an authoritarian social worker*

COMMENT

It may be assumed that an authoritarian service-user is likely to look up to you as a figure of authority and that if you do not live up to these expectations they may well challenge you. Authoritarian service-users may become aggressive if they are not treated according to their expectations and sceptical of your practice if they do not think that you share the same cognitive disposition as them. An authoritarian social worker may be inclined to judge service-users in a negative way if they are perceived to be different to them. Intolerance and lack of person skills may characterise such a person. A number of compli-cations may result from the combination of characteristics. An authoritarian service-user and a non-authoritarian social worker may clash over their differing expectations over appearance and punctuality. An authoritarian personality may admire a neat, tidy image hoping that everything runs according to schedule. A non-authoritarian social worker may dress in a casual way and have a laissez-faire attitude to punctuality. This may produce interpersonal conflict. A similar series of conflicts may result from a non-authoritarian service-user and an authoritarian social worker, with a tense relationship as the service-user misses appointment schedules. Authoritarian service-users and social workers may get along with each other but there is always the danger that there will be a conflict of interests with other service-users and social workers who do not share the same values.

> RESEARCH SUMMARY
>
> *The media have drawn attention to the recent death of 'Baby Peter' and considerable publicity has become associated with this case. Since the death of Maria Colwell in 1973, the following children have lost their lives in situations where prejudicial attitudes were allowed to be expressed: Stephen Meurs, Jasmine Beckford, Kimberley Carlile, Victoria Climbié (online: www.guardian.co.uk). This appears to indicate how important multiagency working is within social work. Since 1997 an emphasis has been placed on organisations within the statutory, private, voluntary and informal sectors coming together and working in partnership in order to provide what Prime Minister Tony Blair phrased as joined-up solutions to joined-up problems. This approach to providing services for children and families is unlikely to work if prejudice and discrimination prevail within wider UK society. In other words, multiagency working needs to be supported by positive attitudes and beliefs within the wider population.*

We have looked at the theoretical background to prejudice, stereotyping and discrimination. In the next section of the chapter we shall consider the stereotyping of older people.

An example of stereotyping relevant to social work practice

Pennington et al. (2002) suggest that there are three characteristic features of stereotyping:

- people are grouped on the basis of highly visible characteristics;
- all members of the group are seen as possessing the same characteristics;
- any person who is perceived as belonging to that group is seen as possessing these characteristics.

How does this apply to older people? It can be argued that the obvious categorising feature for this group would be age. As soon as an individual reaches a particular age, for example around 65 years, they become identified as being an older person. Every older person is then seen as being part of a single, homogenous group possessing a range of common characteristics. Every member of this group is then attributed with associated characteristics, and the stereotype is created.

What is the stereotypical image of an older person? Slater and Gearing (1989) identify several commonly held assumptions about older people as summarised below:

- They are inevitably in a state of physical and mental decline.
- They are beyond the age at which personal change, for example changing lifestyle to improve physical health, is a realistic aim.
- Their memory difficulties are a result of senility.
- Their needs are very different from those of a younger person, for example they need constant assistance and/or protection.
- They do not have the same feelings as younger people, therefore, for example, it is acceptable to make decisions for them without consultation.

- If they are old then they must be unhealthy.

- They are beyond the age of listening to advice about diet and exercise and therefore there is no need to talk with the older person about these subjects.

- Their needs are straightforward and practical rather than complex and emotional.

ACTIVITY 3.7

If you were a social worker working with older people what might interest you about Slater and Gearing's (1989) work?

COMMENT

In Activity 3.1 you were asked to consider how your attitude changed upon being told that the activity was nothing other than a number trick. You may have started to notice how your attitude to the activity changed upon realising how the thoughts were produced in your mind. Similarly, many older people begin to believe in their stereotypical image because this is the message they are directed to accept. The consequence for social workers may be that it becomes difficult to work effectively with older service-users. Difficulties in relation to low self-esteem occur as a result of a self-fulfilling prophecy as older people begin to define old age according to what society expects old age to be.

If we adapt Pennington et al.'s (2002) work to explain why older people may experience prejudice, it can be argued that prejudice occurs because of the highly visible characteristics that distinguish older people as a particular social group. A further significant factor is that all members of the group are seen to be in possession of the same characteristics. This means that an older person has to possess these characteristics to be defined as old. The prejudice that they may encounter is a product of considering them as a category of person as opposed to being a unique individual.

How true are stereotypical images of older people?

Horn and Donaldson (1976), Clayton and Birren (1980) and Banyard (2002) have drawn attention to some of the realities of ageing. It is true that the mind changes with age but these changes are not necessarily negative. The above authors have drawn attention to what improves through age. It can be argued that social awareness intensifies as one ages and that this can contribute to older people having better social skills. The above authors have also emphasised that mathematical, verbal and conceptual ability can improve through age.

If one emphasises that there are benefits to the ageing process this can be a way of avoiding the negative stereotypical images that have become associated with older people. In our society stereotypes of older people can appear on a daily basis. The consequence of these stereotypes may mean that older people are unwilling to work with social workers either because of anger or fear. They may expect a social worker to judge them in the same way that the rest of society judges them. This means that stereotypes of older people have adverse effects on individuals as well as the social worker/service-user relationship. In order to avoid the consequences of stereotyping it becomes essential that you work in as congruent a way as possible with older service-users if you are to achieve the levels of best practice that are ideal.

RESEARCH ACTIVITY

Over the next week or so try to be aware of the assumptions that may be made about older service-users. How often are these assumptions confirmed and how often are they proven wrong?

C H A P T E R   S U M M A R Y

This chapter has demonstrated that attitudes can be defined in a number of ways. It has also been argued that the factors influencing attitude formation are many and varied and that the extent to which attitudes are likely to be put into effect varies according to complex variables. Fishbein and Azjen's (1975) 'Theory of Reasoned Action' exemplifies this point. It states that attitudes are acted upon according to a combination of individual beliefs alongside interpretations of what others value to be significant. In other words a strong attitude that is valued by the individual's respected social circle is likely to produce noticeable forms of behaviour. As an example, a social worker positively valuing inclusion and realising that his or her colleagues endorse the concept of equality of opportunity is more likely to put this attitude into effect.

The chapter has also given some explanations for stereotyping. A stereotype may be formed according to the individual's state of mind. It may also be a product of social circumstances. It may also be created when circumstances covary. It can be argued that an individual's stereotypical attitudes can be extremely resistant to change so it is important to raise awareness of the positive attributes of those sectors of society who experience negative stereotyping. The chapter has exemplified the stereotypical view of older people within our society by means of which 'old age' is seen in negative terms. It is often when we talk to older people about 'what it is like to be old' that we see a much more realistic picture of 'old age'. This may then mean that we are able to begin to appreciate the consequences of relating to older people in a stereotypical way.

Self-assessment questions

3.1 What does Fishbein and Ajzen's (1975) 'Theory of Reasoned Action' state?

3.2 What are the two main factors in the 'Health Belief Model'?

3.3 What are the three levels of oppression according to Thompson (1997)?

FURTHER READING

Malim, T and Birch, A (2000) *Introductory psychology*. London: Palgrave Macmillan.
Look for the sections within the book dealing with attitude formation and stereotyping.

Thompson, N (1997) *Antidiscriminatory practice*. Basingstoke: Macmillan.
A useful text that looks at how oppression is a complex combination of personal, cultural and societal factors.

Chapter 4

Psychology and mental illness

Introduction

'Don't worry!' the nurse grinned at me. 'Their first time everyone's scared to death.' I tried to smile but my skin was tight like parchment. Doctor Gordon fitted two metal plates on the side of my head. He gave me a wire to bite. I shut my eyes. There was a brief silence, like an in-drawn breath. Then something bent down and shook me like the end of the world. 'Wheee-wheee-whee' it shrilled, through an air of crackling blue light and with each flash a great bolt drubbed me till I thought my bones would break and the sap fly out of them like a split plant. (Sylvia Plath, 1963, p151)

All of us here are like rabbits hippity hopping through our Walt Disney World. We're not here because we're rabbits. We'd be rabbits wherever we were. We're here because we can't adjust to our rabbithood. We need a good strong wolf like the nurse to teach us our place. (Ken Kesey, 1962, p55)

The two quotations from Sylvia Plath and Ken Kesey say something about the concern that has existed over the incarceration of the mentally ill. It has been argued that the 'rabbits' Kesey writes about need appropriate 'client-centred' care as opposed to the 'punishment' outlined by Sylvia Plath. This chapter explores these themes by discussing the concepts of 'normal' and 'abnormal' behaviour. We shall look at the causes and consequences of mental illness and consider the example of schizophrenia by investigating its symptoms, diagnosis and treatment. The chapter considers biological and social explanations of mental illness as a means of illustrating the range of professionals who can offer support and guidance to service-users with mental health needs.

After reading the chapter you should be able to:

- identify whether mental illness can be accurately defined as 'abnormal' behaviour;
- describe the categories of mental illness;
- explore some of the ways of treating mental illness;
- contextualise your learning with the specific example of schizophrenia.

Defining mental illness

ACTIVITY **4.1**

What is your own understanding of the term 'mental illness'?

It could be suggested that the moral of Ken Kesey's *One Flew Over the Cuckoo's Nest* is that mental illness is deviant behaviour for which there is no alternative explanation. This definition of mental illness has interested psychologists for a number of reasons:

The answer to the question 'what is mental illness?' is more complex than it might initially appear. You might have thought along the lines of mental illness being a 'disease' that affects the mind. It may be true to say that there are some conditions affecting the mind that appear to be like a disease. 'CJD' can be understood as being a 'disease' affecting the mind. The condition appears to be something that is initially outside the brain that some-how 'infects' the brain producing 'mad' behaviour. Nonetheless there are complications with this definition of mental illness. There are many exceptions to the rule that mental ill-ness is caused by something existing outside the brain, entering the brain and infecting the brain. In fact most well known mental illnesses cannot be explained in this way. There is no 'schizophrenia' virus. There are no bacteria single-handedly producing 'manic depression'. We might say that mental illness is 'inexplicable behaviour' but there are many of us who behave in an inexplicable way yet we are not considered to be 'mad'. The difficulty of defining what is meant by the term 'mental illness' is not a problem of the meaning of the words in isolation. It is more of a problem of what the words mean in tandem. This theme will be explored through the chapter.

- the definition is not made complicated by medical, technical or scientific jargon hence it provides an understandable explanation of the concept;

- this explanation of mental illness introduces the notion of 'deviant behaviour' or behav-iour that is considered to be 'abnormal'.

This last point is particularly important because many people see the distinction between 'mental health' and 'mental illness' as being synonymous with the distinction between 'normality' and 'abnormality'.

It follows that if we are going to define mental illness in terms of 'abnormal behaviour' we need to know what constitutes 'abnormal behaviour' in the first place.

What do you understand by the term 'abnormality'?

As with the concept of mental illness, there is no agreed definition of 'abnormality'. Golightley (2004) explains the categories of mental illness under bio-medical and bio-psychological models. Explanations of abnormality could come into one of the following four categories:

- *behaviour that deviates from statistical norms;*

- *behaviour that deviates from social norms;*

- *behaviour that is maladaptive;*

- *feelings of personal distress.*

Think about your own definition of abnormality in relation to the following definitions.

Behaviour that differs from statistical norms

This definition, 'abnormal behaviour' includes behaviour that is rarely seen in the general population, that is it is not 'the norm'. For example, the majority of the general population can be perceived to eat breakfast, lunch and dinner as their main meals each day. If we use this definition of abnormality, anyone eating significantly less or significantly more than this would be perceived as being 'abnormal'. If we think about this definition a little more we might ask about a number of inconsistencies. What about the person who has a gastric ulcer and who is advised to eat little and often: are they 'abnormal'? Obviously not, so this is a problem with this particular explanation of abnormality. We can also see a difficulty with the definition if we consider the example of 'intelligence'. Is someone with an IQ significantly higher than 'the statistical norm' abnormal? Again this is not the best way of describing 'high intelligence' so there are limitations to this definition of abnormality.

Behaviour that deviates from social norms

Abnormal behaviour may be defined as being determined in relation to the accepted norms or conventions in society. In other words, what is considered to be 'abnormal' is what deviates from these norms and conventions. As with the previous section there are difficulties with this definition of abnormality. The main objection is that social norms are socio-historically relative. This means that what may be considered to be 'abnormal' at one time or in one culture may not be abnormal at a different time or in a different culture. To exemplify this argument, homosexuality was at one time generally considered to be a sign of abnormality because it constituted a deviation from the sexual norms and conventions of society. In contemporary society, although some individuals would still see homosexuality as being abnormal, the social norms suggest that homosexuality is not abnormal behaviour but that it is merely an alternative sexual practice.

Behaviour that is maladaptive

This explanation of abnormality moves away from defining abnormality in relation to social or statistical 'norms'. Behaviour is seen as being abnormal if it has adverse effects on the individual or on society. According to this understanding of abnormality, alcoholism would be seen as being abnormal because of its harmful physical and psychological effects on the individual and on family and friends. Although alcoholism may also be perceived as being statistically and socially abnormal it is the emphasis placed on the maladaptive nature of the behaviour that distinguishes this definition from those of the previous two categories.

Feelings of personal distress

We see a distinct change of emphasis from the focus on 'behaviour' in the first three definitions of abnormality to the importance of 'subjective feelings' in this final category. Here abnormality is not a reflection of deviant behaviour but is defined in terms of 'personal distress'. Although unhappiness is a common human emotion, it is unusual for extreme unhappiness to completely take over someone's life. In other words, being unhappy all the time can be perceived to be abnormal behaviour.

It can be argued that none of these definitions is entirely clear or without problems. This is an important point to bear in mind when studying mental illness and it has been the focus of some considerable debate in this area. The crux of this debate is whether or not we can diagnose and treat mental illness if we cannot define what it is in the first place.

The difficulties that apply to defining 'abnormality' are manifest if one attempts to clarify what is meant by the word 'normality'. It could be argued that normal behaviour is based upon the following characteristics:

- having an accurate perception of reality;
- being able to be realistic about our capabilities and about how we interpret the world around us;
- being aware of motives and feelings so that restraint is shown over involuntary urges if and when necessary;
- having some appreciation of self-worth;
- being able to channel energy into 'productive' activities.

It could also be argued that many of the above characteristics are more of an ideal than characteristics governing most people's behaviour. It may also be suggested that one can only appreciate what is defined as 'normal' behaviour by having some idea about what is meant by the term 'abnormality'. This in turn means that if we are able to understand what it is like to be 'abnormal' how can we ever claim to be completely 'normal'?!

Categories of mental illness

Now that we have looked at what we mean by normal and abnormal behaviour we can look at what actually constitutes a 'mental illness', that is we can begin to look at how it is categorised. This section begins by explaining the difference between 'neurosis' and 'psychosis'.

Neurosis and psychosis

You have probably come across these words before in everyday language, such as the 'neurotic person' or the 'psychotic killer'. But what exactly do they mean?

The most obvious difference between them is that the neurotic person knows that they are behaving in an unorthodox way whereas the psychotic person does not. For example, someone suffering from an obsessive-compulsive disorder in which they find themselves continually washing their hands will be aware that this is not a 'normal' thing to do; they will realise that something is not right.

For a psychotic person such as someone with schizophrenia, this awareness is lacking. In effect, they have lost touch with reality as a schizophrenic may live with their own version of reality. As a consequence they do not see their behaviour as being strange; in fact it is perfectly normal behaviour for the reality in which they are living.

What challenges might you experience if you were working with service-users with mental health needs?

COMMENT

An immediate challenge is the nature of mental illness. We have previously said that this term refers to a complex range of needs. These needs can vary across individuals. It may be argued that the only certain aspect of mental illness is its uncertainty. This poses challenges for the professionals who work with those who are mentally ill. We have also said that another major challenge with mental illness is that the condition cannot be explained by the scientific model that is used to explain other illnesses. There do not appear to be definite causes and cures for many mental illnesses. This means that we need to think about mental illness in a different way to other medical conditions. As well as meeting the needs of service-users who are mentally ill, we may need to alter our own perception of medical problems and their solutions.

Table 4.1 offers a summary of these two categories of mental illness.

Table 4.1 *Neurosis and psychosis*

Neurosis	Psychosis
Part of the personality is affected	The whole personality is affected
It is possible to identify with common cultural values	The person is removed from conventional cultural values
Exaggerated behaviours are evidenced	Unconventional behaviours are evidenced
Causes can be identified	The cause is not necessarily known
Psychological therapy can help	Psychiatric application of medicine is used to treat the individual

Table 4.1 reveals a range of specific differences between neurotic and psychotic disorders. Examples of neurotic disorders include anxiety, phobias, obsessive behaviour and some forms of depression and psychosomatic disorders, that is physical symptoms that have no apparent physical cause. In contrast, the psychoses include schizophrenia and some forms of depression.

It can be suggested that mental illness can be broadly divided into 'neuroses' and 'psychoses', but that these categories are considered to be too broad to be of diagnostic use, that is to identify the specific mental disorder underlying an individual's 'abnormal' behaviour. What is needed is a much finer classification of mental illness, a classification that allows us to diagnose mental illness simply and accurately.

Further classification of mental illness

Table 4.1 provides a classification of mental illness giving you an idea of the variety of mental illnesses or disorders that can be identified. Table 4.2 provides a more detailed list of subcategories within each of these broader categories.

Table 4.2 *Mental disorders*

Disorder	Examples
1 Disorders first appearing in childhood	Hyperactivity, eating disorders
2 Organic mental disorders	Alzheimer's, effects of toxic substances
3 Psychoactive substance use disorders	Drug abuse
4 Schizophrenia	Simple schizophrenia, paranoid schizophrenia
5 Delusional (paranoid) disorders	Feelings of persecution, suspicion
6 Mood disorders	Depression
7 Anxiety disorders	Panic disorders, phobic disorders
8 Somatoform disorders	Conversion disorders, hypochondriasis
9 Dissociative disorders	Amnesia, multiple personality
10 Sexual disorders	Sexual identity, sexual performance
11 Sleep disorders	Chronic insomnia, narcolepsy
12 Factitious disorders	Munchhausen syndrome
13 Impulse control disorders	Kleptomania, pathological gambling
14 Personality disorders	Antisocial behaviour, narcissism
15 Conditions not attributable to a mental disorder	Marital problems, occupational problems

---

RESEARCH ACTIVITY

If there are any of the mental disorders that you do not understand spend some time on the Internet researching what they are.

ACTIVITY 4.4

Table 4.2 refers to 'Munchhausen syndrome'. This disorder is characterised by habitual presentation for hospital treatment for an apparently acute illness. The 'patient' is able to provide plausible evidence for having the disorder but all of these plausible details are false. Why is it difficult to accept that this type of behaviour is evidence of illness?

COMMENT

The American sociologist Talcott Parsons (1967) popularised the notion of 'the sick role'. Parsons argued that we are likely to accept that someone is 'sick' if they fulfil particular role expectations. For example, the sick person ought to stop work. They also ought to seek medical help so that they can get better. In other words we have a 'role' in our mind that we expect the sick person to follow. If the sick person does not follow our expectations of this role we are less likely to accept that they are sick in the conventional understanding of the word.

> **COMMENT** *continued*
>
> *A service-user who has Munchhausen syndrome may be perceived as contradicting key aspects of the sick role. They may be seen as 'feigning illness' as opposed to being legitimately 'sick'. This is because someone with Munchhausen syndrome may be viewed as being unwilling to get better. The judgement may be made that someone with Munchhausen syndrome is 'deviant' as opposed to being ill.*

Treating mental illness

> **ACTIVITY 4.5**
>
> *Imagine that you are a social worker and you are presented with a service-user who is complaining of constant feelings of apprehension, a tendency to overreact, an inability to relax, headaches, dizziness and difficulty making decisions. You decide on the basis of these symptoms that your service-user is suffering from an anxiety disorder. What would you do next? How should your service-user be treated?*

> **COMMENT**
>
> *You may have thought that it is important to make your service-user take drugs in order to ease the above symptoms but it is important to be aware of the range of methods that are available and can be used to treat the symptoms of mental illness. The next section of this chapter looks at some of the therapies that are available for the mentally ill.*

The therapeutic methods available for treating those who have mental illnesses generally fall into one of three categories, psychological, psychiatric or physical. A good working definition of the difference between psychological and psychiatric therapy is that whereas the former therapy does not apply drugs, the latter is frequently based upon drug therapy. Within both of these categories there are a variety of techniques that reflect the 'schools' of psychology that we looked at in Chapter 1.

Table 4.3 illustrates this distinction between psychological and physical methods and provides examples of each.

Table 4.3 *Therapeutic techniques*

Psychological	Physical
Psychoanalysis	Psychotherapeutic drugs
Behavioural therapies	Electro-convulsive therapy
Cognitive behavioural therapies	Psychosurgery
Humanistic counselling	
Eclectic approaches	

Let's look briefly at each of these therapeutic techniques, focusing initially on the psychological methods.

Psychological therapies

Psychoanalysis

Psychoanalytical therapy claims that mental disorders arise as a result of the unresolved conflict between the components of the individual's personality. This conflict is unresolved because it is 'unconscious' or 'repressed', in other words the individual is not aware of its existence. If we are unaware of the existence of 'conflict' then it stands to reason that we are unable to do anything about it.

The aim of psychoanalysis is to bring this conflict into one's conscious awareness so that it can be dealt with and ultimately resolved. This is a long-term process involving techniques such as 'free association' (or talking about whatever comes to mind), 'dream analysis' and 'hypnotherapy'. All of these techniques enable the individual to become aware of conflicts that in some cases date back to early childhood.

Once these conflicts are brought into awareness they can then be 'worked through' until the individual's 'problem' is resolved.

Behavioural therapies

In Chapter 1 we saw that behaviourists regard human behaviour as a series of learned responses to external stimuli. Abnormal behaviour is seen as a particular example of learned behaviour, that is one that is maladaptive.

Taking the example of a phobia, a behaviourist explanation would suggest that the phobic person has previously learned to associate the feared object with negative consequences. The aim of behavioural techniques is to 'unlearn' this negative association through techniques such as a 'systematic desensitisation'.

This therapy was introduced in Chapter 1. If we recall, the technique works by substituting the learned response of 'fear' for the alternative response of 'relaxation'. By teaching the individual to relax the phobic object can then be introduced gradually until a stage is reached when the individual can face the object without experiencing any fear. The person has then been 'desensitised' to the object in a 'systematic' way.

Cognitive-behavioural therapies

Behavioural techniques such as systematic desensitisation tend to focus almost exclusively on maladaptive or 'abnormal' behaviour and pay little if any attention to the individual's thinking or reasoning processes.

Cognitive-behavioural therapies attempt to combine both behaviour modification techniques and procedures aimed at identifying and changing negative or maladaptive beliefs.

This means that if a therapist is working with an anxious service-user he or she would approach the problem from the following two complementary angles.

The individual might be taught relaxation techniques, that is behavioural methods, in order to cope with anxiety symptoms such as panic attacks if and when they happen. In addition, the therapist would try to resolve the negative and/or irrational beliefs held by the service-user that could be precipitating the panic attacks in the first place.

By combining these two approaches the therapist is able to deal with the immediate problems of the panic attacks and also to probe more deeply into the reasons behind these attacks to enable the service-user to appreciate the psychological basis of their problem.

Humanistic counselling

Humanistic counselling is based on what is known as 'the phenomenological approach' as individuals are seen as possessing a natural tendency towards growth and self-fulfilment.

Within this framework mental illness is understood as arising out of 'frustration' as a result of circumstances 'blocking' the individual's progress towards fulfilling their potential. This means that the goal of humanistic therapy is to try to get the individual 'back on course' in terms of psychological development.

The therapist's role is to help the individual to explore his or her own thoughts and emotions. It is thought that this will enable the individual to arrive at solutions to particular problems. This will then result in the resolution of psychological difficulties. Through a process of self-disclosure and self-examination a new perspective is offered. It is argued that the consequence leads to a change in their maladaptive or abnormal behaviour.

Eclectic approaches

This involves combining techniques from each of the main psychological approaches to therapy to provide a comprehensive 'all round' therapeutic framework tailored to the service-user's specific needs.

One particular situation in which an eclectic approach can be used is in the case of 'family therapy'. The rationale behind this type of therapy lies in the belief that individual problems are often caused or exacerbated by communication or relationship difficulties within the family. These difficulties mean that individual therapy is of limited value because, after each therapeutic session, the service-user returns to the 'disturbed' family situation and is then back to 'square one'.

In family therapy the whole family meets with one or two therapists who observe the interactions and relationships within what is known as 'the family system'. In this way each family member can be made aware of how the individual relates to the others and how this interaction may be contributing to the family's problems.

Physical therapies

So far we have looked briefly at psychoanalytic, behavioural, cognitive-behavioural, humanistic and eclectic approaches to therapy. These are only a small selection of the many techniques available within each of the 'psychological' categories. The common factor with all of the categories is the emphasis on non-invasive treatment. The next section of the chapter considers what are usually referred to as the 'physical' therapies for treating mental illness. Physical therapies are characterised by their 'invasive' nature. This term means that the therapies involve some form of medical intervention, from the administration of drugs through to major surgical procedures.

This next section of the chapter considers three of the most influential and popularised physical therapies:

- psychotherapeutic drugs;
- electro-convulsive therapy;
- psychosurgery.

Psychotherapeutic drugs

This group of drugs was seen as a major breakthrough in psychiatric care when first discovered in the 1950s. Until then severely mentally ill individuals were often physically restrained, for example in straightjackets, as there was no other way of controlling their behaviour. With the advent of psychotherapeutic drugs, 'challenging' behaviour could be controlled more effectively and patients could be discharged from hospital more quickly.

The three main categories of psychotherapeutic drugs are:

- anti-anxiety drugs;
- anti-psychotic drugs;
- antidepressants.

Anti-anxiety drugs
These drugs are used to reduce anxiety and they are commonly known as 'tranquillisers'. They work by depressing the action of the nervous system, thus relaxing the individual and relieving tension. The addictive nature of the drugs began to be appreciated in the early 1980s and they now tend to be seen as a short-term measure to be used when the individual is suffering from particularly stressful circumstances. They work by depressing the action of the nervous system thus relaxing the individual and relieving tension.

Anti-psychotic drugs
These drugs are most commonly used in the treatment of schizophrenia. They work to restore chemical imbalance within the brain, which is believed to be one of the causes of schizophrenia. A difficulty with this form of drug therapy concerns the side effects of the drugs that can vary from one individual to another.

Antidepressants

This group of drugs is used to change the mood of depressed individuals, hence their name. Like the anti-psychotic drugs, antidepressants work by restoring the imbalances in the brain which are believed to underlie the symptoms of depression. Although psychotherapeutic drugs do alleviate the behavioural symptoms of mental illness this does not constitute a 'cure'. Antidepressant drugs do not necessarily remove the causes of depression. For this reason psychotherapeutic drugs should ideally be used in conjunction with some of the therapeutic approaches previously discussed.

Electro-convulsive therapy

You may have heard of this particular treatment before; the popular image tends to be like something out of a horror movie, with strong electric currents being sent through the individual resulting in massive convulsions. ECT is only used today in cases of severe depression when all other treatments have failed. The individual is now given a short-acting anaesthetic together with a muscle relaxant, which prevents the convulsive spasms previously associated with this method of treatment.

There are side effects such as memory loss but these may be minimal and it can be argued that there are some benefits associated with ECT. If you were suffering from extreme depression then you might think that a slight memory loss was a small price to pay for the improvement in your psychological condition.

Psychosurgery

Psychosurgery involves the destruction of selected areas of the brain in order to alleviate severe psychological and behavioural symptoms. As with ECT this particular form of treatment has received negative publicity especially in films such as *One Flew Over the Cuckoo's Nest*.

The procedure still remains controversial. Early procedures were seen to relieve symptoms of mental illness but the consequence was that other cognitive faculties could be adversely affected. More modern techniques and refinements have lessened the risk of this side effect and, as with ECT, the procedure is viewed as being helpful in treating severely depressed patients who have tried all other forms of treatment without success.

ACTIVITY 4.6

Why might a social worker object if a service-user was going to face psychosurgery?

COMMENT

One of the key social work roles in the National Occupational Standards is to support individuals to represent their needs, views and circumstances. It could be argued that allowing a service-user to have psychosurgery may go against this principle because the side effects of the treatment may mean that the treatment causes negative effects for the service-user. This produces an ethical dilemma for a social worker. How can one allow a therapy if it is going to lessen the service-user's life chances?

So far we have looked at mental illness and abnormal behaviour in general. The final section of the chapter looks at a specific example of mental illness: schizophrenia.

The example of schizophrenia

In this section we are going to look at schizophrenia as an example of a psychotic mental disorder. We shall be looking at the symptoms of schizophrenia, at possible explanations of its cause and at treatments that may be used to alleviate its symptoms.

Symptoms of schizophrenia

The first point to consider is that the term 'schizophrenia' actually refers to a group of disorders and not to one single condition. Generally speaking schizophrenia is characterised by a severe disorganisation or disruption of the individual's personality, a distorted view of reality and an inability to function efficiently in everyday life.

Some of the more specific symptoms are presented below.

Disturbances of thought and perception
This is often reflected in the way that schizophrenic patients speak and write. For example, in writing, the words may be combined into small phrases that make sense but when expressed as a sentence they become completely meaningless. For example:

> *I am referring to a previous document when I made some remarks that were facts also tested and there is another that concerns me my daughter she has a lobed bottom right ear, her name being Mary Lou.* (Atkinson et al., 1987, p618)

These disturbances of thought can also be apparent in the form of delusions or misinterpretations of reality. The most common delusions are beliefs that external forces are controlling the individual's thoughts and actions.

Disturbances of perception
During an acute episode of schizophrenia the individual often reports that the world appears to be different. Colours can seem to be brighter or noises can seem louder. This misinterpretation can also affect self-perception. In extreme cases the individual loses their power of self-recognition because everything seems to be different. They might see their hands as being too large or too small and their eyes may be seen as being out of place on their face.

Disturbances of affect
Individuals with schizophrenia often do not show standard emotional responses. They may laugh at something most people would find sad or they may show no emotional response whatsoever.

Withdrawal from reality
During a schizophrenic episode the individual will tend to withdraw from others and become absorbed in his or her inner thoughts or fantasies. This state of absorption can be so intense that the person does not know what day of the month it is or even where he or she is at the time.

Decreased ability to function

The range of symptoms that can be experienced by the schizophrenic person can affect their ability to function normally in everyday life. The consequence can be that they might not be able to hold down a job, their interpersonal relationships may suffer and their personal hygiene can become neglected.

Causes of schizophrenia

Now that we have looked at some of the characteristics of schizophrenia we need to consider its aetiology. What causes people to develop these symptoms?

It can be argued that the answer to this question seems to be that it is a condition that is caused by the interaction of a range of factors, such as heredity, physiological changes in the brain, social circumstances and environmental influences. The following sections look at some of the genetic, physiological and socio-environmental explanations for schizophrenia.

Genetic theories of schizophrenia

Golightley (2008, p28) defines schizophrenia as a neuropsychiatric disorder. Gottesman and Shields (1982) have found that the incidence of schizophrenia within the general population is usually 1 per cent. These two researchers have also identified that there appears to be a genetic causative component to schizophrenia. These findings are summarised in Table 4.4.

Table 4.4 *Risk factors in schizophrenia*

Relationship	Risk
Unrelated person	1%
Child of one schizophrenic parent	13%
Child of two schizophrenic parents	46%
Sibling	10%
Nephew/niece	3%

Gottesman and Shields initially discovered that the closer the relationship between the schizophrenic person and the family member, the greater the likelihood that the family member will develop the symptoms of schizophrenia. It is significant that for each of the family relationships within Table 4.4 the risk factor is higher than that of the general population. This is most apparent for the child of two schizophrenic parents. These results suggest that there is a genetic influence in the development of schizophrenia. This is supported by Golightley (2008, p29), who records that two-thirds of people diagnosed with schizophrenia never recover from their symptoms.

We can see further evidence of this in studies of twins, both identical and fraternal. Fraternal twins are no more genetically similar than any other siblings so accordingly there is no immediate reason to presume that there ought to be a reason why they would be more prone to developing schizophrenia. Conversely Gottesman and Shields found this risk factor to be slightly higher at 14 per cent but what is especially interesting is that when we look at identical twins the picture is very different. Identical twins possess identical genetic make-up and therefore if there is a hereditary factor in the development of schizophrenia we might expect it to be most apparent in these twins. The Gottesman and Shields study found that the risk factor for identical twins rose to 46 per cent, compared with 14 per cent for fraternal twins. This is clearly a significant increase and it would seem to confirm the theory that schizophrenia can be predicted according to genetic factors.

A question that could be asked is if there are twins who are genetically identical why don't we get a 100 per cent risk factor? If one twin develops schizophrenia then surely it should be inevitable that the second twin will also develop the disorder. Why doesn't this happen?

ACTIVITY *4.7*

Why do you think the risk factor for identical twins is not 100 per cent?

COMMENT

One reason may be that social and environmental factors also seem to play a part in the development of schizophrenia. Although the twins do have an identical genetic make-up they do not necessarily have the same life experiences and therefore it is not inevitable that they will both develop schizophrenia. These socio-environmental factors have been explored to some extent in what have become known as 'adoption studies'. These studies involve assessing the risk factor of children of schizophrenic parents who are adopted into and raised by non-schizophrenic families. By doing this the genetic and social factors can be separated and isolated in order to assess the contributory effects of each.

What we tend to find is that the 46 per cent risk factor identified by Gottesman and Shields (1982) for children of schizophrenic parents is substantially reduced (to approximately 35 per cent) when the child is adopted into a non-schizophrenic family. This appears to confirm the view that there is more to the development of schizophrenia than pure genetic background.

Physiological theories of schizophrenia

If we accept Gottesman and Shields' findings it is important to consider how genetic components can actually account for the symptoms of schizophrenia. In order to do this, researchers have worked on the assumption that this hereditary factor leads to a biochemical imbalance in the brain and that this imbalance then produces the symptoms associated with schizophrenia.

One of the most influential 'biochemical imbalance' theories is known as the 'dopamine hypothesis'. This is discussed by Saunders and Gejman (2001) in relation to experimental progress in schizophrenia genetics research. Dopamine is a chemical substance known as a 'neurotransmitter'. It carries information around the brain and it is believed to be involved in the regulation of emotion. The 'dopamine hypothesis' suggests that an excess of dopamine causes the symptoms of schizophrenia. This occurs at the point where nerve cells connect with one another with the consequence being the display of schizophrenic behaviour. Most of the evidence for this theory is derived from two main sources:

- The drugs that are effective in relieving the behavioural symptoms of schizophrenia are also known to reduce the levels of dopamine in the brain. This would appear to suggest that there is a link between the behavioural symptoms of schizophrenia and the levels of dopamine in the brain.

- It has also been observed that amphetamine abuse produces psychotic symptoms closely resembling those of schizophrenia. The important point about this observation is that amphetamines are known to increase dopamine levels in the brain.

In addition to these two findings, it has also been found that treating amphetamine abusers with the same anti-psychotic drugs used in the alleviation of schizophrenia relieves the psychotic symptoms of abuse. All of this appears to suggest that if dopamine activity within the brain is increased, for example with amphetamines, we see the appearance of schizophrenic symptoms. Likewise, if dopamine levels are decreased with anti-psychotic drugs, the symptoms are alleviated. Thus dopamine levels do seem to play a key role in the aetiology and manifestation of schizophrenia.

Social theories of schizophrenia

Golightley (2008, p29) draws attention to the social aspects of schizophrenia. As well as the hereditary and biochemical influences on the development of schizophrenia it is also important to consider socio-environmental influences. Two factors are especially important:

- the role of the family;

- the effects of stress.

Family therapy concentrates on analysing the relationships and communication patterns within the family environment. In some ways there are links to the transactional analysis that was outlined in Chapter 2. During the 1950s and 1960s a vast amount of research was carried out into communication and relationship patterns within the families of schizophrenic individuals. The aim of this research was to identify the types of attitudes and behaviours within the family that might contribute to the development of schizophrenia. The influence of social factors on schizophrenia is acknowledged by Golightley's (2008, p29) finding that one-third of people diagnosed with schizophrenia completely recover upon receipt of appropriate care. It can be argued that both medical and social factors are important.

Three dysfunctional communication patterns influencing schizophrenia are described below.

The double-bind communication

This particular form of communication was initially popularised by Gregory Bateson (1972). The child is placed in a 'no-win' situation by contradictory messages that are both verbal and non-verbal. This communication comes from the child's parents. The parents do not necessarily realise that they are doing this but, for the child, the only way of dealing with the confusion caused by such messages is to withdraw into their own world away from everyone else. In this situation family therapy may be of help in that it is possible that there will be a raised awareness of the dysfunctional nature of this communication and of its harmful effects on the child.

Pseudomutuality

This term means that the relationships within the family environment are rarely favourable or 'mutual'. It can be argued that all of us can experience a degree of ambivalence or negativity towards family members at some time, whether this is anger, jealousy or even hatred. It can also be argued that it is important that this ambivalence is resolved if we are to maintain positive relationships within the family. The difficulty arises when this ambivalence is not dealt with and when there is a level of 'pretence' about the quality of family relationships. This is what Wynne et al. (1977) refer to as 'pseudomutuality' or 'false mutuality'. This suppression of negative feelings together with the pretence that everyone is 'OK' within the family may lead to confusion. It is argued that children are especially sensitive to this social relationship. As with the occurrence of 'double-bind' it has been suggested that the symptoms of schizophrenia may be a response to these feelings of confusion. It can be argued that the resulting sense of helplessness that can arise from not knowing how best to deal with the pseudomutual relationships may produce schizophrenic behaviour. These social causation factors are supported by Golightley (2008, p34).

Marital schism and marital skew
'Marital schism' refers to the situation in which the parents' relationship is poor but they stay together 'for the sake of the children'. What we then tend to see happening is that the children are treated well by the parents but that each individual parent may communicate negative messages about each other to the children. In contrast to this situation, 'marital skew' refers to a family environment in which one parent denies the very real negative qualities of his or her partner. Moreover, these qualities are patently obvious to the child. The argument runs that both of these social situations are conducive to producing schizophrenic behaviour.

If we apply the work of Gross (2005) it is possible to see why it has been claimed that marital schism and marital skew produce schizophrenic behaviour. Gross applies Albert Bandura's social learning theory in explaining this situation. The theory has its origins in behaviourist psychology. It is sometimes thought of as referring to the ways in which humans imitate the behaviour they are exposed to. As an example, it may be inferred that someone growing up in a violent household may become violent as well because they will learn that this is how they ought to behave. Bandura's argument is more refined than this simplistic assumption. It is proposed that if an individual is to imitate or 'model' other forms of behaviour there has to be a relationship of emotional attachment. It follows from this argument that if a child has a close emotional attachment to his or her parents the 'mixed messages' that appear in both situations of marital skew and marital schism may produce behavioural traits that could be labelled as being 'schizophrenic'.

ACTIVITY *4.8*

Read the following scenarios and then decide which is an example of marital schism and which is an example of marital skew.

1 *'Person A' may tell the child that 'Person B' is a 'bad person'. Then to contradict this completely, 'Person B' arrives home and is very good to the child.*

2 *'Person A' is aggressive, even violent, and because of this 'Person B' always agrees with everything 'Person A' says, just to keep the peace. One night, when it is cold and raining heavily outside, 'Person A' suggests that it is a pleasant night for a stroll. Because 'Person B' is frightened of 'Person A' the whole family goes out for a walk.*

> **COMMENT**
>
> 1 This is an example of marital schism. What is the child to think in this situation? Not surprisingly the child is likely to become very confused about who is good and who is bad. When this happens we can see the conditions falling into place whereby the child may eventually withdraw into his or her own non-contradictory and non-confusing world.
>
> 2 This is an example of marital skew. On the one hand the child can see that it is not the weather for 'a stroll' but on the other hand he or she is being told that they have to go out walking. Once again the child is caught in a state on confusion and if this state is not resolved the temptation may be for the child to withdraw into a world over which he or she has some control.

You may have experienced some or all of these situations at some time in your childhood, or even now. If this is the case why don't we all develop schizophrenic symptoms as a consequence? It can be argued that the difference in the above activity is that the child's state of confusion is long-lasting and that it can seem never-ending. Our own experience of such social situations may be limited in comparison to these examples. If an individual is continually faced with confusing and contradictory attitudes this can place enormous stress on the individual. The consequences can in turn produce serious problems for the individual's physical and psychological health.

This relationship between stress and schizophrenia may mean that those individuals who are born with a genetic predisposition towards developing the mental disorder may find that the illness is 'triggered' later in life either by a specific stressful event, such as bereavement, or by a series of more general stressful circumstances, such as dysfunctional family communication. This explanation of the way in which these components interact is referred to as the 'diathesis-stress model' of mental illness. This idea was initially popularised by Thomas Holmes and Richard Rahe (1967) and developed in relation to the connection between stressful life events and the onset of schizophrenia in adults. Golightley (2008, p35) refers to these causes of mental disorder as 'psychosocial' factors. Holmes and Rahe's 'Social Readjustment Rating Scale' provides an estimated measure of an individual's 'stress level' on the basis of the number of stressful events they have experienced over the previous six months to one year. It has been shown that schizophrenic patients often report having experienced more of these stressful events than non-schizophrenic individuals and this would seem to support the argument for a relationship between stress and the onset of schizophrenia.

It can also be argued that we need to be careful in interpreting these results as it may be the case that people who experience the symptoms of schizophrenia will perceive life events to be more stressful than 'normal' individuals. However, if this study is taken together with studies of the physiological changes associated with stress then the diathesis-stress model does seem to be credible.

This means that the aetiology of schizophrenia is complex. The associated symptoms are the end product of an interaction involving a variety of factors, including genetic composition, family situation and levels of stress. Additional factors, such as sex, socio-economic status, environment, for example urban or rural, race and social support have also been identified as being influential in the development of this disorder.

Having reached these conclusions, what then is the most effective treatment for schizophrenia?

Treatment of schizophrenia

In an ideal world the treatment of schizophrenia would be an eclectic combination of both physical and psychological therapies. This would mean that anti-psychotic drugs would be used in conjunction with individual and/or family therapy. This would have the effect of treating the immediate situation, the symptoms and the underlying problem(s) giving rise to this situation in the first place.

The reality is that we do not live in an ideal world. This can mean that this eclectic approach is often seen to be impractical because of the limited resources available to the professionals working with those who have mental illness. Individual psychotherapy is not always cost-effective because of the time involved whereas anti-psychotic drugs are cost-effective and do appear to alleviate the immediate problem. The consequence can be that it is these drugs that are frequently the preferred approach in treating the disorder. It may be argued that the difficulty of this approach is that it does not actually 'cure' the problem because it merely serves to relieve the schizophrenic symptoms.

C H A P T E R   S U M M A R Y

This chapter has identified that mental illness is a complex area of study both in its definition and in its classification. The chapter began by discussing whether it is possible to define mental illness as 'abnormal behaviour'. This section of the chapter argued that the difficulties in defining what is 'normal' and 'abnormal' behaviour mean that it is incorrect to categorically state that 'mental illness is nothing other than abnormal behaviour'.

The chapter then discussed the categories of mental illness that are of interest to psychologists. These categories of mental illness can be treated in various ways. These practical treatments are often of particular interest to social workers working with service-users with mental health needs. The therapies represent a combination of psychological and physical techniques. It can be suggested that the most effective way of treating mental illnesses such as schizophrenia is to address the genetic, biochemical and social components that constitute the aetiology of such illnesses. The two quotations introducing the chapter say something about the concern that has existed over the incarceration of the mentally ill. This chapter explores these themes by discussing the concepts of 'normal' and 'abnormal' behaviour. It may mean that there exists something that is more positive than a 'strong wolf' to frighten the mentally ill into conforming to what the rest of society expects. It can be argued that this has been a past approach to treating those with mental illness. It can also be suggested that it is an approach that ought to be confined to the past.

Self-assessment questions

4.1 Describe three ways in which neurosis differs from psychosis.

4.2 Compare and contrast the psychoanalytic and behavioural approaches to treating mental illness. What is meant by an 'eclectic' therapeutic approach?

4.3 What are the three main categories of psychotherapeutic drugs?

FURTHER
READING

Golightley, M (2008) *Social work and mental health*. 3rd edition. Exeter: Learning Matters.
A highly recommended text investigating the implications of mental illness for social work practice.

Gross, RD (2005) *Psychology: The science of mind and behaviour*, 5th edition. London: Hodder Arnold.
An excellent text in terms of depth and detail.

Malim, T and Birch, A (2000), *Introductory psychology*. London: Palgrave Macmillan.
A helpful text. Accessible material is related to social care settings.

Chapter 5
Child psychology

This chapter will begin to help you to meet the following National Occupational Standards:

Key Role 1: Prepare for and work with individuals, families, carers, groups and communities to assess their needs and circumstances.

- Prepare for social work contact and involvement.
- Work with individuals, families, carers, groups and communities to help them make informed decisions.

Key Role 2: Plan, carry out, review and evaluate social work practice with individuals, families, carers, groups, communities and other professionals.

- Interact with individuals, families, carers, groups and communities to achieve change and development and to improve life opportunities.
- Work with groups to promote individual growth, development and independence.

Key Role 3: Support individuals to represent their needs, views and circumstances.

- Advocate with and on behalf of individuals, families, carers and communities.

Key Role 5: Manage and be accountable, with supervision and support, for your own social work practice within your own organisation.

- Work with multidisciplinary and multi-organisational teams, networks and systems.

Key Role 6: Demonstrate professional competence in social work practice.

- Work within agreed standards of social work practice and ensure own professional development.
- Contribute to the promotion of best social work practice.

It will also introduce you to the following academic standards as set out in the social work subject benchmark statement:

3.1.1 Social work services and service-users

The social processes (associated with, for example, poverty, unemployment, poor health, disablement, lack of education and other sources of disadvantage) that lead to marginalisation, isolation and exclusion and their impact on the demand for social work services.

3.1.4 Social work theory

Research based concepts and critical explanations from social work theory and other disciplines that contribute to the knowledge base of social work including their distinctive epistemological status and application to practice.

The relevance of psychological and physiological perspectives to understanding individual and social development and functioning.

3.1.5 The nature of social work practice

The factors and processes that facilitate effective interdisciplinary, interprofessional and interagency collaboration and partnership.

The subject skills highlighted to demonstrate knowledge include:

3.2.2 Problem-solving skills

3.2.2.3 Analysis and synthesis

Introduction

*He thought his happiness was complete when, as he meandered aimlessly along, suddenly he stood by the edge of a full-fed river. Never in his life had he seen a river before – this sleek, sinuous, full-bodied animal, chasing and chuckling, gripping things with a gurgle and leaving them with a laugh, to fling itself on fresh playmates that shook themselves free, and were caught and held again. All was a-shake and a-shiver – glints and gleams and sparkles, rustle and swirl, chatter and bubble. (*Kenneth Grahame, 1995, p20).

The saying goes that it is important to make sure that you never lose your sense of childish wonder about the world. It could be suggested that the quotation by Kenneth Grahame is steeped in wonder, the delightful fascination upon discovering that the world can be a wonderful place that is filled with creativity and vitality. Most people would probably endorse that a child should experience the world as a place of wonder so that they develop into adults who can look back on their childhood experiences with both affection and a *wild imagination* (Ingleby, 2006, p135). To reword the saying: give me the child and you will see the person. In other words there exists a critical link between the experiences of childhood and the characteristics of adulthood.

This chapter looks at some of the contributions that have been made by psychology in relation to understanding children and their development. The five main aims of the chapter are to:

- identify what interests key psychological perspectives about child development;

- analyse how the child's personality develops over time;

- analyse how the child's thought processes develop;

- analyse how the child's linguistic ability develops;

- critically appraise whether nature or nurture determines a child's identity.

The work of Karin Crawford and Janet Walker (2003) is applied to the chapter. It is anticipated that its content is likely to be of particular interest to social workers and other health/care professionals who wish to work with children.

Perspectives explaining child development

Crawford and Walker (2003, p18) draw attention to the number of perspectives that can be applied to understanding how children develop. These perspectives represent a combination of psychological, biological and sociological understandings of what influences child development.

This section of the chapter introduces some of the key ideas within some of these perspectives. We have identified and explored the key psychological paradigms in Chapter 1 of the book. This section introduces what these perspectives say about child development in particular.

'Developmental psychology' is concerned with understanding how individuals develop over time in relation to their surroundings. It could be argued that all of the main psychological perspectives we discussed in Chapter 1 have some interest in child development. There follows a summary of what aspects of individual development are of interest to each of the perspectives. Before proceeding let us recall a working definition of each of the perspectives we looked at in Chapter 1.

ACTIVITY **5.1**

Write out a working definition for behaviourism, humanism, psychodynamic theory, cognitive theory and biological psychology.

COMMENT

- *Behaviourism is particularly concerned with the impact that external environmental factors have on the mind.*

- *Humanism theorises that each individual is unique and that the human mind understands the surrounding environment in an original way.*

- *Psychodynamic theory proposes that the human mind is a combination of conscious and unconscious thoughts. Moreover, the conscious mind is a small component of the wider unconscious mind.*

- *Cognitive psychology is interested in what happens after a stimulus but before a reaction appears in the mind.*

- *Biological psychology is interested in the impact that hormones and chromosomes have on thought processes.*

Behaviourist explanations of child development

Behaviourist psychologists such as Skinner and social learning theorists such as Bandura are particularly interested in how cognitive processes are influenced by the surrounding environment. Crawford and Walker (2003, p23) argue that Skinner considers child development as being *the acquisition of behaviours which are learned through responses to experiences*. Of central importance to this explanation of child development is the idea that the individual child is not producing independent behaviour. In this theory behaviour is viewed as being a response controlled by the rewards and punishments within the individual's environment.

Albert Bandura is also interested in the ways in which the environment influences behaviour. As Crawford and Walker emphasise, Bandura considers *cognition, or thought, to be a significant factor in the person's development*. This means that *social learning theories consider the influence of values, beliefs, reasoning, self-determination, emotions and thought on the learning process*. All of these factors are crucially linked to the environment so it follows that what is understood to be a positive or negative environment produces thoughts within the child's mind that will be in turn positive or negative.

Joseph is nine years old. He lives with his parents in a high-rise flat in a run-down inner-city area. Joseph's parents are both unemployed. His father is a heavy drinker and regularly physically abuses Joseph's mother when he comes in from the pub on a Friday night. Joseph's father has established a strong emotional bond with his son. He takes him out to the boxing club on Saturdays. Joseph's father used to be a keen boxer when he was younger and Joseph wants to be 'just like his dad' when he gets older.

What do you think would interest Skinner and Bandura about Joseph's personality development? How is this theory of child development relevant to social work practice?

Skinner and Bandura have both popularised the idea that child development is linked to external factors. Both psychologists would accept that 'Joseph's' thoughts are likely to be determined by his environment. Joseph lives with a father who is physically aggressive to his mother and moreover he has a strong emotional bond with his father. According to Bandura this means that Joseph is likely to 'model' or imitate his father's behaviour. The theory is of interest to social work practice because it suggests that in such circumstances it is entirely understandable for a child to be removed from an abusive household. What is also of interest is the complexity that this process is likely to cause, especially in consideration of the relationship existing between the father and his son. It may be correct to remove a child from an abusive family environment but when there is such a close emotional bond between parent(s) and child, the intervening role of social workers may be perceived in a very negative light.

Humanist explanations of child development

In Chapter 1 we identified that humanists such as Carl Rogers are interested in how individuals make sense of their environment. The environment is regarded as being important in that it is seen as being a major factor that shapes the individual's personality. It may also be argued that within the humanist perspective an emphasis is placed upon the environment influencing rather than determining personality. Whereas behaviourism may be interpreted as arguing that the individual is determined by the environment, humanism suggests that personality is shaped in conjunction with the environment. This means that humanists accept that the child develops by being influenced by its environment, but because the child's personality is unique it evolves in relation to its environmental circumstances. This argument is reflected in the following quotation from *On Becoming a Person*:

> *Experience is, for me, the highest authority. The touchstone of validity is my own experience. No other person's ideas, and none of my own ideas, are as authoritative as my experience. It is to experience that I must return again and again, to discover a closer approximation to truth as it is in the process of becoming in me.* (Rogers, 1961, p23)

In other words, if we are to look to find the 'truth' of child development we must find out the nature of the child's experience of development. Rogers would argue that if the child has been unable to achieve their aspirations they are likely to be characterised by the 'would/should dilemma' outlined in Chapter 1. This will produce feelings of anxiety and impede personality development. Conversely, if the child interacts with the environment in a positive manner and its aspirations are realised, the result is likely to be a balanced 'anxiety-free' personality.

CASE STUDY

Dominic is married and has three daughters aged five, seven and nine. Dominic has always wanted to have a son and although he loves his three daughters he would ideally have liked to have had two sons and one daughter. Dominic realises that he is fortunate to have three healthy children but he is concerned about the number of occasions he seems to lose his temper with his youngest daughter. He was so sure that this third child was going to be a boy. Dominic wonders whether he should talk about these feelings as up until now he has kept these thoughts to himself.

ACTIVITY 5.3

What would interest humanists about Dominic?

COMMENT

Dominic is exemplifying the 'would/should' dilemma. He 'would' like to have a son but he knows that he 'should' be grateful for his three healthy children. The tension within these thoughts is causing Dominic to lose his temper with one of his daughters. Humanists recommend that we should resolve dilemmas like this if we are to develop our innate sense of goodness. This means that Dominic needs to accept that he cannot change what has happened and that losing his temper will do nothing other than exacerbate the situation.

Psychodynamic explanations of child development

Psychodynamic psychology, as popularised by the work of Sigmund Freud, proposes a dual model of the mind. The argument goes that the mind is a combination of conscious and unconscious thoughts. As we saw in Chapter 1, the theory proposes that whereas we are aware of conscious thoughts we are much less aware of unconscious thoughts. This may mean that we are unaware of why we behave in a particular way. Our unconscious thoughts are released and determine particular ways of behaving. As with humanism, psychodynamic theory acknowledges the importance that the environment has in influencing one's thoughts. It is argued that the manner in which a child progresses through the stages of development identified in Chapter 1 determines the thoughts that appear within the mind. This means that if the child experiences physical/emotional crises at any stage in their development the mind is likely to be adversely affected. As we saw in Chapter 1, it is important to remember that although psychodynamic theory can be interesting it is not necessarily accurate. Gross (1999, p917) adapts Popper's criticism of psychodynamic perspectives by saying that *they are unfalsifiable and, therefore, unscientific*. In other words psychodynamic therapy can be applied but there needs to be the awareness that the therapy is not likely to offer every possible answer to every possible question.

CASE STUDY

Sarah came to see her social worker because her boyfriend had broken off the relationship. Her whole world had fallen apart since Philip had told her they were finished two nights ago and Sarah thought of little else in the intervening time. She was unable to sleep and she began to 'binge eat'. Sarah became distressed and anxious and wanted advice about what she should do. She had previously had a relationship with a boyfriend who had been a heavy drinker and had abused her verbally. Philip seemed different. He seemed kind and Sarah had moved into his flat. She was aware that other women found Philip attractive and at first she was pleased about this, but later worried that she did not have the ability to hold his attention. Sarah's mother had always warned her about the unreliability of men and she claimed to be 'at her wits' end'.

ACTIVITY 5.4

How would a psychodynamic psychologist explain Sarah's development?

How might these ideas be useful for social work practice?

COMMENT

A psychodynamic psychologist would interpret Sarah's 'binge eating' as a sign that she has an oral fixation. This may be interpreted as suggesting that Sarah has experienced some kind of trauma between the ages of birth and 1. In applying this perspective to understanding Sarah's behaviour it is also of interest that Sarah has an obvious tension in her relationships with men. This is indicative of a 'phallic fixation'. It suggests that there may have been a traumatic happening in Sarah's life between the ages of 3 and 6. A psychodynamic psychologist might interpret Sarah as having an unresolved 'Electra' complex. It could be proposed that the relationship between Sarah and her mother and father at the ages of 3–6 may have generated this Electra complex. It could also be suggested that this is an 'as if' argument! In other words it is 'as if' all of this has happened!

Nonetheless, for social workers working with emotionally distressed service-users an explanation is offered for behaviour that may seem to be inexplicable. This in itself is useful for social work practice. At the very least psychodynamic theory arouses debate and reflection about how and why the child's personality traits emerge and develop.

Cognitive explanations of child development

Cognitive psychologists such as Piaget and Vygotsky are interested in how the child's thinking processes develop over time. Both psychologists acknowledge that the environment has an important influence on how thinking processes evolve. According to Piaget and Vygotsky, children are likely to be impeded in their cognitive development if they do not have the positive environmental stimuli that are necessary for them to develop complex thinking processes. This means that both psychologists are interested in the factors that enable a child's mind to develop from birth onwards. The key question asked by both Piaget and Vygotsky is *what is happening within the child's mind when it is receiving particular stimuli?* For Piaget the ideal is that the child reaches the stage of formal operations where it is capable of 'reversible' or complex problem solving (when a child can 'see in its head' that 3 − 1 is the same as 1 + 1). Vygotsky uses the term 'Zone of Proximal Development' (or ZPD) to describe when a child has reached its cognitive potential. Both cognitive states depend upon how the child interacts with the environment stimulating its cognitive processes.

CASE STUDY

Petra is 11. She has an older sister and a younger brother. Her father teaches in a primary school and her mother is a university lecturer. The family live in a pleasant house with a garden and a playroom. Petra has always been looked after by her parents. From an early age Petra's mother ensured that she followed a timetable of activities that was designed to stimulate her physical, intellectual, emotional and social development. Petra went to playgroup at 2, nursery at 3 and began school at 4. From an early age Petra seemed to be capable at English and maths. She could do 'sums in her head' by the age of 6. Every evening Petra had 'mammy time' before bed where she worked on English and maths activities with her parents. She started to have piano lessons at 7 and gained an excellent mark in her 11+ exam. Her parents have pushed for Petra to be educated in one of the few remaining traditional grammar schools in the locality. Petra says that when she grows up she wants to teach in a university just like mammy does.

ACTIVITY 5.5

What would interest Piaget and Vygotsky about Petra's development? What is significant for social work practice about Petra's development?

Piaget would claim that Petra has reached formal operations and is capable of reversible thought by the age of 11. She has done well in the 11+, an examination that is designed to test 'reversible thinking processes'. It could be argued that Petra's thought processes have developed because of the stimulation offered by her surrounding environment. Her thought processes have been nurtured from an early age. Vygotsky would be interested in the 'scaffold' of people supporting Petra's development. Her parents are both involved in teaching and have socialised with her during what they call 'mammy time' to make English and maths a part of her world. This would propel Petra towards reaching her 'ZPD' (to use Vygotsky's term). It can be argued that what becomes significant for social work practice is the impact that a child's environment has on their cognitive development. It is true to say that in the case of Petra, she also needs to be in possession of the innate cognitive ability to respond to her environmental stimuli. With the exception of genetic engineering there is little that can be done to influence this capability but it is apparent that a positive nurturing, learning environment can be created and that this is a responsibility that social workers must be aware of.

Biological psychological explanations of child development

Psychologists such as Gerald Davison, John Neale and Ann Kring apply a biological basis to their work. Davison, Neale and Kring (2003) propose that blood, injury and injection phobias are crucially linked to family background. This means that if someone has this specific phobia there is a 64 per cent chance a blood relative will also have the condition. In other words, biological psychologists are interested in the relationship that exists between the thoughts within the child's mind and the individual's hormonal and chromosomal characteristics. These biological components are considered to be the critical factors in determining a child's thought processes.

Bruce was surgically castrated as a baby boy. His gender was changed through biological and social processes. He was renamed Brenda and brought up as a girl. Through plastic surgery he was physically turned into a female. At puberty he was given female hormones in order to assist the process of gender change.

What would interest biological psychologists about Bruce's development? What might be significant for social work practice about the above case study?

Those applying biological perspectives such as Milton Diamond would be interested in the extent to which Bruce's biological maleness could be engineered into femaleness. If one accepts that identity is on the whole determined by genetic inheritance it can be argued that even with surgery, hormonal injections and socialisation, one cannot change what has been biologically determined. If this theory of child development is accepted (and there is increasing evidence to suggest that identity is linked to biological factors, for example Toates (2000)), social workers need to be aware that child development is critically influenced by genetic inheritance and hormonal development.

The development of personality

Crawford and Walker (2003, p30) emphasise that personality *development is influenced by and the product of a number of different and interrelated processes or systems*. This means that if social workers are to gain an accurate understanding of the child's personality it is important to have some knowledge about what is referred to as the 'whole child'. This section of the chapter discusses some of the key factors that influence the development of the child's personality.

Think about your own personality. What would you say are the critical factors that have shaped your personality?

Upon being asked this question, many people immediately think that their parents have had an enormous impact upon their personality. How many times do we hear it said that 'she's just like her mother' or 'he's just like his dad'. We often associate our personality with our physical characteristics and we frequently assume that these characteristics have come from our parents. Moreover, we may think that our level of kindness or the extent of our lack of kindness is a product of the traits that we have inherited from our parents. We may also think of how our family background, our relationships, our school and our peers have influenced our personality.

Although a child's personality emerges over time it is important to acknowledge that the processes begin prior to birth. Crawford and Walker (2003, p35) emphasise the importance of social workers needing to understand the relationship between *structural inequalities such as poverty* and the impact that these factors have upon the development of the unborn child. In other words, the mother's nutritional intake affects the growing foetus and this in turn has an impact upon the child's personality.

Once the child has been born, the first two years of life are acknowledged as being especially important (Crawford and Walker, 2003, p36). Psychologists such as Piaget have acknowledged that babies are born with a number of innate reflexes but it is important to emphasise that many aspects of personality are learned as the child interacts with its environment. The environment is an important factor influencing the formation of the child's personality but Crawford and Walker (2003, p37) emphasise the importance of understanding that a complex range of variables affect the child's personality from the ages of 2 to 6. These factors include *the child's genes, their temperament, their emotional and social development, the impact of the family, the context in which the family live and the culture in which the child grows up*.

Psychologists interested in child development have drawn attention to the importance of the relationship of 'attachment' between a child and its parents. The concept of 'attachment' has been popularised by John Bowlby (1953, 1969, 1973, 1988). It refers to the idea that mothers and children have an instinctive need for physical and emotional closeness within the early life of the child. Bowlby has referred to the separation of a child from its mother as an occurrence of 'maternal deprivation'. The consequences of this occurrence are regarded as leading to 'delinquent behaviour' and 'mental health issues'. Indeed Crawford and Walker (2003, p44) refer to the 'affectionless psychopathy' that results if the child perceives that they have lost their 'mother's love'.

Bowlby's work has not been without criticism. It could be argued that although a child may need to form an 'attachment' it does not necessarily mean that it has to make this attachment with its mother. This means that Bowlby may have focused too much on the child–mother relationship to the detriment of relationships with the child's father and its siblings. Another difficulty that has been commented on by Rutter (1981) is that in emphasising the importance of the mother's emotional warmth, other factors such as chronic lack of basic needs and stimulation through play may have been neglected.

Nonetheless, it can be argued that despite these difficulties, attachment theory is of importance to social workers. Crawford and Walker (2003, p46) emphasise that social workers need to be aware of as many factors as possible in relation to *the nature, form and development of relationships* and one of these factors is indeed the extent to which the child experiences relationships of attachment.

As a child moves into 'middle childhood' (between the ages of 5 and 12) it is likely to experience 'qualitatively different' physical, intellectual, emotional and social experiences (Crawford and Walker, 2003, p54). This is an important phase for the development of the child's personality because middle childhood may reinforce the experiences of early childhood. In Chapter 1 we identified that Freud regarded middle childhood as being a time of 'latency' with an emphasis on the development of social and intellectual skills. In relation to this point, the above authors (2003, p56) make reference to the work of Erik Erikson who refers to the ages of 6 to 12 as being a time during which the child reconciles feelings of 'industry' (or competence) in relation to feelings of 'inferiority'. In other words it is important for the child to be able to develop new intellectual and social skills such as reading, writing and the formation of friendships. Erikson also argues that it is particularly important that the child is supported at this stage of its life so that it does not develop a sense of inferiority or incompetence. If this happens, it may mean that the child's 'damaged personality' restricts its development into adolescence and adulthood.

ACTIVITY 5.8

How might Bowlby's attachment theory and Erikson's 'industry/inferiority' theory be applied to explaining adolescent behavioural problems?

COMMENT

Challenging behaviour in adolescents can be explained in a number of different ways. The cause may rest with the individual person or it may be down to a number of complex occurrences that combine together and produce a series of challenging behaviours. It may be argued that if an adolescent is overly insecure because of a lack of 'child attachment', this feeling may result in challenging behaviour. In other words, it is the experience of insecurity that produces the challenging behaviour. The child may become overly aggressive in order to release 'pent-up feelings' or its personality may become increasingly introspective. It may also be the case that if a child develops particularly strong feelings of inferiority this can be expressed in adolescence in a number of challenging ways. The individual may become overly reclusive or develop 'self-destructive' behaviour such as 'self-harming' with the root of this behaviour being the sense of inferiority experienced and reinforced in middle childhood.

The development of thought processes

In outlining the development of the child's cognitive processes Jean Piaget and Lev Vygotsky have similarities and differences. The extent of their differences and similarities is open to debate. They are both cognitive psychologists interested in how the child's thought processes develop. The extent to which they acknowledge the influence of environmental factors on thinking processes is again open to debate. Whereas Piaget has been accused of being perceived as focusing on 'inner thought processes' Vygotsky is understood as placing an emphasis on 'potential' and the environmental factors that lead to this potential (Malim and Birch, 1998). This may be argued as being a significant difference between these two cognitive psychologists.

Piaget's theory of cognitive development

Piaget sees the intellect in terms of 'schemata' and 'operations'. Schemata are understood as being internal representations or 'cognitive plans' existing in the mind. According to Piaget a baby is in possession of a number of schemata, for example a 'looking schema', a 'grasping schema' and a 'sucking schema'. In other words its instinctive behaviour has a cognitive origin.

Piaget argues that these basic schemata are different to 'operations' or 'higher mental structures'. As outlined earlier, these cognitive processes have the characteristic of 'reversibility'. In other words they are more complicated mental processes. For Piaget, this kind of thinking is not acquired until middle childhood.

ACTIVITY **5.9**

In Chapter 1 we identified that Piaget proposes that there are a number of stages of intellectual development. Write out these stages of cognitive development and give an outline of how the main characteristics of each stage of development relate to your knowledge of children and young people.

COMMENT

Stage 1: Sensorimotor stage (0–2)

The child experiences the world through immediate perceptions. The phrase 'out of sight, out of mind' applies. This means that thinking is dominated by the 'here and now'.

Stage 2: Preoperational stage (2–7)

As the child's linguistic ability improves it is capable of 'symbolic' thought. This means that the child can use words to refer to people and objects. This more developed thought is limited by 'egocentrism' and 'centration'. Egocentrism means that the child is unable to see the world from any other point of view but their own understanding of it. Centration means seeing one feature but ignoring the wider reality. In Chapter 1 we said that a child might think that a ton of lead is heavier than a ton of feathers because the child has only thought of the objects as lead and feathers and not realised that both weigh a ton!

Stage 3: Concrete operations (7–11)

Piaget argues that at this stage of cognitive development the child begins to solve more complex problems. This provides the ability to 'decentrate'. It means that the child becomes less egocentric and is more capable of seeing the viewpoint of others. This stage of cognitive development is called 'concrete operations' because the child still needs to use practical objects in order to solve problems. A question such as Joan is taller than Susan; Joan is smaller than Mary; Susan is smaller than Mary; who is the smallest? will pose difficulties for the child at this stage of cognitive development unless there is access to a pen and paper to solve the problem. (It may pose problems with adults as well as children!)

Stage 4: Formal operations (11+)

Piaget argues that 'formal operations' mark the beginning of abstract thinking. Problems can be tested in the mind and more complex ideas can be formed.

Vygotsky's idea of cognitive development

It can be argued that Lev Vygotsky differs from Piaget in that he is understood as placing a particular emphasis upon the importance of the role of other knowledgeable people in cognitive development. Thought processes should not be portrayed as being confined to the mind (and it could be argued that this is the impression one might get of Piaget's work even if this was not his intention). Vygotsky argues that the developing child forms a framework or 'scaffold' of influential peers who have a fundamental bearing on the child's cognitive development. It is this influence of others that is considered to be essential in forming individual cognitive concepts and problem-solving skills.

Vygotsky also emphasises the importance of linguistic development in solving problems. It is argued that it is through talking about problems that individuals organise perceptions, with three elements considered to be especially important:

- action: the ways in which individuals respond to problems;

- language: the ways in which individuals talk about problems;

- social settings: the places in which individuals are able to develop their problem-solving skills.

We have referred to the ZPD (or Zone of Proximal Development) earlier and this is an important concept within Vygotsky's account of cognitive development. The ZPD is regarded as being the area between actual development and potential development. It is argued that the individual's potential development can be realised through positive inter-action with others. As an example, a musically gifted child who teaches him or herself to play the piano will cross the ZPD into potential development with the help of piano lessons from an influential music teacher.

ACTIVITY 5.10

How might Piaget and Vygotsky's account of cognitive development be useful for social workers?

COMMENT

It can be argued that if Piaget and Vygotsky's work is combined it offers a powerful explanation of the child's cognitive development. This account is particularly useful for social workers working with children in a role that is designed to help the child's physical, intellectual, emotional and social development. Both psychologists emphasise that cognitive development depends upon how a child interacts with its environment. Through providing appropriate developmental activities the child's cognitive processes ought to develop accordingly. Through their explanation of how the child's thought processes develop, Piaget and Vygotsky offer guidelines that may be used to structure developmental activities. As an example, two-year-old children often enjoy making lines of objects such as cars. Piaget would argue that this schema needs to be nurtured and developed through play so that the child's mind can develop further schemata. Social workers who are involved with structured play with children can use these theories to aid the child's development. As well as making lines of objects, the child's mind can be stimulated through varying this activity (for example making objects appear and disappear and threading beads on a piece of string). These activities enable the child to develop its cognitive schemata. Vygotsky's work is important because it draws attention to the critical impact that an individual's social circle has in developing the mind. This means that it is important for a social worker to be aware of the link that exists between the service-user's cognitive development and their peer group.

The development of language

In the previous sections of this chapter we have seen that the environment plays a particularly important role in the development of personality and thought processes. It can also be argued that the child's environment has a critical bearing on its linguistic ability.

This point is emphasised by Bernstein (1961). Bernstein argued that there are two important forms of speech pattern, an 'elaborated code' and a 'restricted code'. Whereas 'restricted code' refers to the limited use of language, 'elaborated code' refers to using words in a creative and original way. For Bernstein, restricted code is characterised by 'basic linguistic conversation' exemplified by simple 'yes' and 'no' statements, closed questions, alongside the limited use of adjectives. Meaning comes more from tone, gesture and other non-verbal/vocal forms of communication. Blunt phrases are used and although the words used in the phrase are restricted, their intonation gives them a particular force. In contrast to restricted code, elaborated code refers to more complicated uses of language. There is the occurrence of detail and images. This leads to the use of metaphor within conversations so that word-games result. The Kenneth Grahame quotation at the start of the chapter is a good example of what Bernstein means by elaborated code. It is 'rich text' overflowing with images and alliteration.

Bernstein argues that the type of language used by the child depends upon the type of environment they experience. In other words if the child's parents use restricted code, the child's conversation will in turn be characterised by restricted code. Likewise a child socialised into a family who use elaborated code will also use elaborated code.

Bernstein's emphasis on the link between socio-environmental factors is also at the heart of Piaget and Vygotsky's account of the child's linguistic development. The difference between the two theorists is neatly summarised by Richard Gross.

> *Piaget's view on language and thought can be summarised as claiming that language depends upon stages of cognitive development. Vygotsky argues that language and thought begin as separate but then come together when the child is about two years old. The significance of this is that by 1962 Piaget had come to accept this view. (Gross, 1992, p373)*

It can be argued that once more it is important to view Piaget and Vygotsky as complementing each other. According to Piaget, language begins as 'autistic' speech. This means that between the ages of 2 and 7 language directed at the self and at others cannot be distinguished. Piaget argues that as the child's problem-solving skills develop, autistic speech is replaced with 'egocentric' speech. Piaget proposes that this type of speech develops around the age of 7. It can be interpreted as meaning that language is used as a way of giving a running commentary on what the child is doing as it tries to make sense of its world. The final stage of linguistic development is 'socialised speech' where the child uses language in many varied complex ways.

Vygotsky's account of speech development in children can be used to complement Piaget's work. The theory claims that that until the age of 2 there are 'prelinguistic thoughts' and 'preintellectual language'. The former are initial perceptions and images. The latter are cries and babbles. The argument runs that when the child is 2-years-old these two areas overlap resulting in verbal thought and rational speech. Vygotsky follows Piaget's argument by then claiming that whereas speech is initially egocentric it then develops into socialised speech. This theory of speech development is summarised in Figure 5.1.

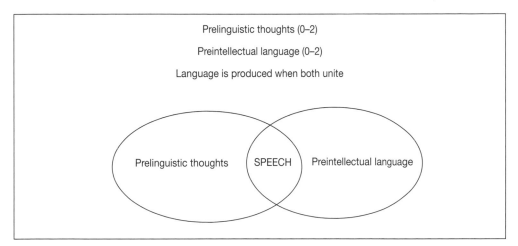

Prelinguistic thoughts (0–2)

Preintellectual language (0–2)

Language is produced when both unite

Prelinguistic thoughts   SPEECH   Preintellectual language

Figure 5.1 *Vygotsky's theory of linguistic development*

A number of debates exist in relation to the development of the child's linguistic ability. Plunkett (1981) argues that a central issue is the discussion that surrounds the extent to which grammar is a 'cognitive function'. In Chapter 2 we identified that Chomsky (1972) argued that children learn to speak because of the possession of a 'Language Acquisition Device'. This cognitive function is considered to be an innate capability. Skinner (1957) adopted a different approach by claiming that speech is an example of social conditioning. It could be argued that the two approaches should not necessarily be seen as unworkable opposites. In other words, linguistic ability may be an innate human cognitive trait, but its development is also influenced by the social factors that are emphasised by Bernstein and Skinner. This produces the basis of the holistic approach to therapy referred to in Chapter 1.

ACTIVITY **5.11**

How might the contributions of Piaget, Vygotsky, Chomsky, Skinner and Bernstein to understanding the child's linguistic development be of use to a social worker working with children?

Piaget and Vygotsky both draw attention to the stages of linguistic development within children. It may seem to be an obvious point but it is important to pay attention to the words that are used when we communicate with children. Both Piaget and Vygotsky acknowledge that 'socialised' adult speech takes time to develop. A social worker working with children needs to acknowledge this idea so that speech can be used in a developmental manner.

It can be argued that Chomsky's idea of a 'Language Acquisition Device' implies that children have an innate propensity for using words. This means that in helping the intellectual, emotional and social development of the child it is important to incorporate 'word activities' into care plans whenever possible.

The work of Skinner and Bernstein is of importance to social work because it draws attention to the social issues within the child's linguistic development. This means that words can be used to create, develop and nurture social relationships. In order to develop best practice it is important for social workers to be able to influence the social worker/service-user relationship as positively as possible by considering the words being used to communicate this relationship. This may mean that it becomes important for social workers who are working with children to spend time aiding and assisting linguistic development.

Chapter 2 applied Koprowska's (2005) work in relation to communication skills. It can be argued that social workers who have a raised awareness of how to develop children's linguistic ability are able to contribute to child development more effectively.

The importance of nature and nurture

This final section of the chapter appraises whether child development is a consequence of nature or nurture. This debate has been of interest to social scientists for a number of years. From the popularity of social learning perspectives through the 1960s, 1970s and 1980s to the contemporary critique offered by biological psychology there is a recurring interest in the link between child development and the influence of nature and nurture.

Biological perspective versus social perspective

We have already identified that the central idea of biological psychology is that genes and hormones shape our thought processes. Likewise, the factors influencing the child's personality development are in turn reduced to genes, hormones and chemical reactions occurring in the mind and body. This means that the child's personality is attributed to internal traits. Malim and Birch (1998, p145) summarise the biological approach by saying that it *studies the relationship between physiological and psychological make-up and the interactive influence of one on the other.*

In contrast to biological psychology, social perspectives on personality development adopt a similar argument to the behaviourists by arguing that the personality is a product of the social environment. One of the most influential studies to have popularised this perspective was carried out by the anthropologist Margaret Mead. Mead studied three social groups in New Guinea in the 1930s, arguing that gender roles were cultural constructions. This is because each social group's expression of male and female identity depended upon shared understandings of what was believed to be appropriate male and female behaviour. Whereas the Arapesh were characterised by non-aggressive affectionate characteristics in both sexes, the Mundugumor were typified by males and females behaving in a masculine aggressive and assertive way. In contrast, the Tchambuli witnessed females being assertive and aggressive and males being gentle, passive and non-assertive. Mead's work appears to support the argument that personality development depends upon social factors. In other words we may be a physical product of chromosomes and hormones but social forces determine the development of the child's personality.

Appraising the argument

In contrast to seeing the child's personality as being a product of either nature or nurture it can be argued that it is more acceptable to propose that any personality is a complex product of both biological and social factors. This avoids reducing the complex components of an individual's personality to a set of 'either/or' variables. This is the central idea of Robert Winston's (2003) work that utilises the developments within genetic science alongside acknowledging the importance of social factors in shaping one's personality. It can also be argued that it is important to 'think outside the box' in order to try to become a 'paradigm shaker'. It is true that the traditional psychological debates have been interpreted as emanating from influential paradigms and that this influence has waxed and waned according to who has been associated with the paradigm. Nonetheless it can also be argued that if psychology is to move forward in understanding human beings it is important to combine ideas from various perspectives so that a holistic awareness of the science of the mind can be achieved. If this approach to the discipline occurs it will ensure that the ideal of Richards (2002) is realised so that psychology is put 'in its place'.

> ### RESEARCH ACTIVITY
>
> *Using the Internet try to identify articles that are attempting to apply holistic approaches to psychology. You might begin by going to a search engine and doing a search under 'holistic approaches to psychology'.*

C H A P T E R   S U M M A R Y

This chapter has discussed the contribution that psychology makes to understanding how the child's personality develops. Each of the main perspectives identified in Chapter 1 has been considered in relation to this theme. To understand how a child's thought processes and linguistic ability develop over time it can be argued that it is important to apply a holistic approach that utilises a breadth of psychological perspectives. This argument has been recommended in appraising whether a child's personality is a product of nature or nurture. It is too simplistic to adopt an 'either/or' approach in relation to this argument because the variables that determine personality can be many and varied. This can in turn assist the practice of social workers working with children because it suggests that the common-sense assumptions that often exist in relation to personality development may indeed be 'common' but they do not necessarily make 'sense'.

Self-assessment questions

5.1 Identify the main perspectives accounting for the development of the child's personality.

5.2 Analyse why Piaget and Vygotsky are claimed to have 'similarities and differences' in relation to the developing child's thought processes.

5.3 Appraise whether a child's personality is a product of either biological or social forces.

FURTHER
READING

Crawford, K and Walker, J (2003) *Social work and human development*. Exeter: Learning Matters.
A useful text that looks at child development in relation to social work practice.

Malim, T and Birch, A (2000), *Introductory psychology*. London: Palgrave MacMillan.
A clearly written text discussing child development in relation to social work practice.

Chapter 6
Psychology and old age

ACHIEVING A SOCIAL WORK DEGREE

This chapter will begin to help you to meet the following National Occupational Standards:

Key Role 1: Prepare for and work with individuals, families, carers, groups and communities to assess their needs and circumstances.

- Prepare for social work contact and involvement.
- Work with individuals, families, carers, groups and communities to help them make informed decisions.

Key Role 2: Plan, carry out, review and evaluate social work practice with individuals, families, carers, groups, communities and other professionals.

- Interact with individuals, families, carers, groups and communities to achieve change and development and to improve life opportunities.
- Work with groups to promote individual growth, development and independence.

Key Role 3: Support individuals to represent their needs, views and circumstances.

- Advocate with and on behalf of individuals, families, carers and communities.

Key Role 5: Manage and be accountable, with supervision and support, for your own social work practice within your own organisation.

- Work with multidisciplinary and multi-organisational teams, networks and systems.

Key Role 6: Demonstrate professional competence in social work practice.

- Work within agreed standards of social work practice and ensure own professional development. Contribute to the promotion of best social work practice.

It will also introduce you to the following academic standards as set out in the social work subject benchmark statement.

3.1.1 Social work services and service-users

The social processes (associated with, for example, poverty, unemployment, poor health, disablement, lack of education and other sources of disadvantage) that lead to marginalisation, isolation and exclusion and their impact on the demand for social work services.

3.1.4 Social work theory

Research-based concepts and critical explanations from social work theory and other disciplines that contribute to the knowledge base of social work including their distinctive epistemological status and application to practice.

The relevance of psychological and physiological perspectives to understanding individual and social development and functioning.

3.1.5 The nature of social work practice

The factors and processes that facilitate effective interdisciplinary, interprofessional and interagency collaboration and partnership.

The subject skills highlighted to demonstrate knowledge include:

3.2.2 Problem-solving skills

3.2.2.3 Analysis and synthesis

Introduction

They umm-ed and they aah-ed and they stared towards the ceiling, chewing pencils to destruction over 16 across.

It was hell out there in the Great Western Suite of the Paddington Hilton in London yesterday as the cream of The Telegraph crossword enthusiasts, plucked from breakfast tables, garden recliners and commuter trains across the land, joined battle in the same room.

The silence was deafening, broken only by the hum of the air conditioning and the throb of brains struggling over 'Inconsistent statement in Pope's document (4)' and 'Bacon could be comparatively audacious (6)'.

Finally, 30 minutes and 24 seconds into the competition, a hand shot up, waving in the air. It belonged to Brian Murgatroyd, aged 66, a retired tax inspector from High Wycombe, Herts, and when his answers were checked, they were all correct.
(www.telegraph.co.uk)

It can be argued that not everyone might automatically assume that the winner of a competition testing mental agility and powers of lateral thinking would be an 'older person'. In other words our national perception of older people is not necessarily as positive as it could be. Within the above extract there is the message that old age and retirement do not necessarily mean the loss of intellect and ability. This chapter considers these themes by looking at 'ageing processes'. The chapter begins by discussing some of the important physical changes associated with ageing. This is because our psychological state of mind is affected by the physical ageing processes in tandem with our individual reactions to getting older.

Upon reading the chapter you should be able to:

- define 'old age' from a number of selected theoretical viewpoints;
- identify theories explaining the process of ageing;
- explore the external signs of ageing;
- explore age-related conditions, focusing on depression and dementia;
- discuss the relationship between age and intellect;
- assess how the memory is affected by ageing processes.

Defining old age

In Chapter 5 we looked at 'theories of development' that attempt to account for psychological change throughout an individual's life. In this chapter we will be focusing specifically on explanations of development in late adulthood, that is on the process of ageing. Before we do this we need to consider the more fundamental question of what constitutes 'old age'. The term is often used in everyday conversation but what exactly does it mean?

ACTIVITY **6.1**

What do you understand by the words 'old age'?

COMMENT

It can be argued that even the developmental theorists who work in this area find it diffi-cult to give an absolute definition of the specific life periods within the life cycle. The term 'age' can have different meanings to individuals as they move through the life cycle. For example, a 6 year old might see their 15-year-old brother or sister as an 'adult' or even as 'old'. Fifteen year olds may consider themselves to be 'adult' when their parents still regard them as 'children'. At the opposite end of the spectrum, some 60 year olds will see themselves as middle-aged, reserving the term 'old' for someone of 75 years or more. This means that 'old' is a relative term; it means different things to different people. You might see someone as being old, whereas someone else might consider the same person to be middle-aged.

It can be proposed that this problem is not restricted to defining 'old age'; it exists regard-less of the 'stage' of life under consideration. The term 'childhood' causes difficulties in this regard because it is not possible to answer conclusively when 'childhood' ends and 'adulthood' begins. It can be suggested that in contemporary western society the transi-tion is usually identified as being somewhere around the late teens when the individual becomes legally defined as an 'adult' in such areas as voting behaviour, driving, sexual activity and so on. The complexity of the situation is put into perspective upon considering that this age of transition does not apply to all contemporary societies and was far from being the case in historical times. This means that definitions of childhood are socio-his-torically relative, and it is this relativity that makes such transitions throughout life so difficult to identify in any objective way.

Theories explaining the ageing process

A number of theories account for the processes involved in physical ageing. This section of the chapter looks at three of these theories. Although there is not a detailed account of the biology and physiology of ageing in this chapter, it is important to be aware of the link that exists between an individual's physical ageing processes and their psychological state of mind. The three specific theories of ageing that are going to be considered are:

- wear and tear theory;
- cellular theory;
- immunity theory.

Wear and tear theory

Klatz and Goldman (1997) argue that Dr August Weismann, a German biologist, first intro-duced 'wear and tear' theory in 1882. It is a theory that is based on the assumption that living organisms are like machines. It proposes that just as machines such as cars 'wear out' with use and time, each human's physiology is affected in a similar way. The theory runs that over time the body accumulates damage from external factors, such as pollution, as well as from internal factors, such as poor diet. By the time old age is reached the body is vulnerable to the ultimate factor that leads to the individual's death.

ACTIVITY **6.2**

What do you think might be a problem with wear and tear theory?

COMMENT

A major problem with the theory is the fundamental assumption that human beings are analogous to machines. Machines cannot repair themselves, whereas human beings have developed a range of mechanisms, such as the regeneration of skin tissue, that allow repairs to be put into effect and the process of wear and tear to be slowed down. This means that the machine analogy and the subsequent wear and tear account of development cannot accommodate the reality of what happens during the process of ageing. It is also inappropriate to compare older service-users to 'machines'. Such a comparison would not take into consideration the potential complexity of the social worker/service-user relationship.

It can be argued that wear and tear theory is too simplistic and too general in claiming that as people get older their bodies wear out. What is required is a theory that attempts to go beyond a superficial level of explanation.

Cellular theory

James (1995) explains that cellular theory investigates how disease arises from micro-organisms within the cells of the body. In particular, the theory is concerned with the ways in which errors in cell division occurring throughout life contribute to the degenerative conditions we see in later years. For example, an 'error' during the process of cell division could produce two faulty cells, which would then divide to form four faulty cells, dividing again to produce eight and so on. Over the course of time these faulty cells will eventually impair the function of the part of the body in which they are to be found.

A second area of interest in cellular theory is the accumulation of toxic substances within the body as it develops into late adulthood. There are two particular explanations of ageing that fall within this category of 'accumulation theories', one involving changes in the body's ability to get rid of metabolic waste and the other relating to changes in what are known as 'collagens'. Some substances such as 'lipofuscin' begin to build up in the body with advancing age. After many years of accumulation this substance begins to form areas of darker pigmentation, or liver spots, on the skin.

Collagen fibres are found in the body, particularly in muscles, joints and bones. With increased age these fibrous proteins become thicker, less elastic and less soluble. Eventually they tend to replace existing tissues. Age-related changes in collagen fibres can be seen in various external signs of ageing, such as wrinkling of the skin, sagging muscles and a tendency for slower healing of cuts and wounds.

Immunity theory

Metchnikoff (2000) has been instrumental in popularising immunity theory. In this theory ageing is explained at a physiological rather than a cellular level. This particular approach to ageing suggests that changes occurring in the body's immune system will eventually result in physical degeneration. More specifically, as the body ages its immune system becomes less efficient so there is an increased chance that harmful cells will not be killed off. These harmful cells then cause damage to the body so that we begin to see the beginnings of degeneration.

There are several variations to this immunity theory of ageing. The first strand of immunity theory is based on the assumption that the immune system is unable to recognise slight deviations or faults in molecular structure and cell characteristics. This means that cells that have undergone mutation and would normally have been destroyed by the immune system are no longer recognised and are allowed to grow and develop in the usual way. This in turn impacts upon the health of the body as a whole.

A second aspect of immunity theory suggests that even though the immune system can recognise these deviations, it is not able to produce enough antibodies to destroy them. The consequence is that although the immune system recognises faults in molecular and cell structure it is unable to effectively overcome these faults.

The final variation of this approach to ageing, the 'auto-immune theory', sees ageing as resulting from the development of antibodies within the body that destroy not only abnormal cells but also those that are normal and healthy. This results in the auto-immune antibodies working in a self-destructive way.

There are several versions of the immune theory of ageing with each one focusing on a different level of functioning within the immune system as a whole. It is important to emphasise that there is no one explanation of ageing that can account for the range of changes that take place throughout the life cycle. We have looked at just three such explanations, wear and tear, cellular and immunity theories, but there are many more.

ACTIVITY **6.3**

What do cellular theory and immunity theory have in common?

COMMENT

All of these theories have one thing in common: they are all trying to account for the changes that we see within our bodies throughout life and particularly within the later years of 'old age'. Some of these changes are going to be relatively superficial, such as wrinkling of the skin, whereas others will be of much greater significance to the person experiencing them. This latter category will necessarily include changes in physical and mental health.

ACTIVITY *6.4*

Why do you think that these theories explaining the ageing process are important for social work?

COMMENT

If you are working with older service-users it is important to be aware of what happens to the body as it ages. In understanding the nature of the ageing process you will be in a better position to give advice and support to older service-users. Although a difference of focus is given in each of the theories accounting for physical ageing it is important for social workers to be aware of the consequences that the ageing process can have for service-users. Ageing is an inevitable process. Despite the difficulties that exist in defining what is meant by 'old age' there is an acceptance that the body ages over time and that this can produce both physical and psychological consequences for service-users requiring social work support. In the UK increasing numbers of service-users are older people. Being aware of how and why these service-users have aged is likely to enhance social work practice through raising knowledge and awareness of this particular group's needs. This reinforces the National Occupational standards requirement of being aware of service-users and their needs in relation to their circumstances.

The external signs of ageing

ACTIVITY *6.5*

List the main major physical changes occurring in older people.

COMMENT

You probably included things like:

- *wrinkling of the skin;*
- *slower movements;*
- *weakening of the bones;*
- *joint pain;*
- *changes in posture;*
- *increased tiredness;*
- *greying hair or hair loss;*
- *loss of teeth;*
- *loss of memory.*

It is important to emphasise that, contrary to some stereotypical assumptions, older people are not usually sick or unhealthy. Although some older people may need care, other older people are very independent. In other words old age does not necessarily have to be synonymous with poor health. In an example survey, Starr and Weiner (1981) carried out a study of the health status of a sample of people between the ages of 60 and 90 and the results were as follows:

- over 70% of people taking part in the study described their health as 'excellent' or 'good';

- 25% regarded their health as 'fair';

- only 3% reported their health as being 'poor'.

Despite these findings, it can be argued that there are a range of physical and psychological changes that can be observed in older people. We have already made reference to the importance of social workers being aware of the physical ageing process. It can also be argued that it is important to be aware of these physical changes because of the potential effect that they can have on the individual's psychological welfare. The next section of the chapter elaborates upon some specific examples of physical ageing.

The skin

Holliday (1995) drew attention to the human ageing process. The most obvious effect of the ageing process on skin is the occurrence of wrinkling. A number of factors contribute to wrinkling including a loss of subcutaneous fat tissue and a loss of skin elasticity. Normal skin cells in an average 70 year old live for only 46 days, compared with about 100 days for a 30 year old. In addition to this shorter life span of older skin cells, the cells themselves are replaced more slowly. Furthermore, the skin loses its ability to retain fluids with age resulting in it becoming dry and less flexible. Spots or darker pigmentation accompany the ageing process and wounds tend to take longer to heal than previously.

Of all the changes that take place with the skin, the most important is the gradual inability to regulate body temperature. With age, people become more susceptible to ill health because they no longer have the physiological ability to adapt to changes in the external temperature. In addition, the loss of the insulating layer of subcutaneous fat together with the decreased capacity of the circulatory system can make older people more vulnerable to the cold. This means that social workers working with older people need to be aware of the importance of ensuring that their service-users wear appropriate clothing, especially in winter.

The hair

Authors such as Johnson (2005) have drawn attention to the physical and psychological consequences of the ageing process. With advancing age the hair in general can become greyer and begin to lose its lustre. For most people the hair continues to thin, with a high proportion of men eventually going bald. Hair loss on the arms and legs may also become more extensive with age. In women a change in the androgen/oestrogen hormonal ratio can have the effect of producing facial hair on the upper lip and chin. Social workers need to be aware that older people can be especially sensitive to their appearance. This means that sensitivity and tact ought to be applied when you are working with older service-users.

The teeth

Many people are faced with coping with the loss of teeth at some point during their life-time, but particularly in old age. Steele et al. (1998) have calculated that by the age of 75, the average person has lost all but 15 of their teeth so dentures become the norm for most people at this time of life.

Posture

Lord et al. (2001) have drawn attention to the link between age and postural stability. For an older person, shrinkage of discs in the spinal column eventually leads to a slight loss of physical stature. Loss of collagen between the spinal vertebrae also causes the spine to bend and this, together with the tendency of elderly people to stoop, often gives the appearance of being even shorter. This may mean that it is important for social workers to be aware of the need to utilise the expertise offered by health professionals such as phys-iotherapists in order to provide holistic therapy to older service-users.

ACTIVITY 6.6

What effects might external ageing processes have on the mind of an older person?

COMMENT

There would not appear to be many people in our society who are looking forward to reaching old age. This might be because of the negative images that are associated with advancing years within western culture. In 1975 Ernest Becker popularised the idea that most of us make psychological attempts to 'deny death' so the physical ageing processes are unlikely to be received well. This can contribute to feelings of low self-esteem, lack of confidence, anxiety and depression within older service-users. It can be argued that the physical ageing process is never curtailed. It is as if one were to try to stop the seasons or the tides of the sea. It is an occurrence that has an inevitable probability. If the ageing process is associated with negative attitudes learned from society there is every reason why this process is likely to have an affect on the minds of service-users. Many older people may begin to think that they are not able to make a positive contribution to society. This can in turn generate a self-fulfilling prophecy where the feelings of low self-esteem that are generated by society become a central aspect of the older person's personality.

Depression and dementia in older people

It is important to emphasise that there is a connection between the physical conditions experienced by an older person and the psychological consequences of such conditions.

Having made this link explicit let us now look in more detail at the occurrence of depression and dementia within the older population.

Depression

Depression within older people can be a consequence of adjusting to chronic illness. The condition may also be a product of a range of other complex factors. It may be a consequence of the pervading stereotypical perception that old age equates with 'social redundancy'. Biebel and Koenig (2004) have drawn attention to the different kinds of depression that exist. This can be either a transient (normal) depression such as we see in the general air of sadness that many people experience following a bereavement, or a prolonged (pathological) depression, which is much more pervasive and self-destructive.

ACTIVITY **6.7**

What do you understand by the term 'depression'?

COMMENT

You may have described any of the following feelings:

- *sadness;*
- *unhappiness;*
- *feeling 'low';*
- *tiredness;*
- *guilt;*
- *hopelessness;*
- *helplessness;*
- *apathy;*
- *loss of memory;*
- *not wanting to 'join in'.*

It can be argued that pathological depression can develop as a response to chronic illness or to the general ageing process. This means that individuals who are unable to cope with the idea of becoming old may develop pathological depression.

In general, older people who are depressed show two main symptoms:

- depressive mood: sadness, guilt, hopelessness and helplessness;
- reduced behaviour: giving up, apathy.

Negativity, limited attention and memory loss, in addition to physical complaints such as indigestion, are also frequently present within those diagnosed as being 'depressed'. As with schizophrenia, biological and socio-cultural factors can contribute to depression in old age. In addition, psychological factors, such as loss of 'sexual drive' with advancing years, can also be influential in the development of this condition. If the depression is severe then there may be excessive guilt, anxiety, hypochondria, delusions, excessive fatigue and suicidal thoughts.

One of the complexities associated with depression is that it tends to 'feed' upon itself. In other words once a person becomes depressed it is very difficult to get them to recognise that new techniques for coping with their difficulties can be helpful. This may mean that when faced with potentially difficult life events depressed older people tend to be less likely to look for 'a way out' of the situation than non-depressed people. Those who are not depressed will ask for advice and take specific action in order to deal with the situation. Depressed people are less likely to do this as their coping strategies may involve emotional outbursts and over-indulgence in food, smoking or alcohol, none of which will change the situation that is causing the problem in the first place.

The previous section of this chapter has described how ageing processes involve external and internal changes within the body, and that these changes can lead to the development of various physical, chronic conditions. It has also been revealed that chronic illness is considered to be a contributory factor to the development of depression and that the symptoms of this condition are emotionally, psychologically and physically wide-ranging.

It is important for social workers to be aware that for some older people, being referred to a social worker may be the 'final straw' that results in depression. The negative image of 'social work' that is often reinforced in the media may in turn add to the sense of depression that is experienced by an older person. The psychological consequences of this depression can then affect interaction to such an extent that anger may be directed towards particular social workers with the consequence being a lack of compliance with professional advice.

RESEARCH ACTIVITY

Using the internet, try to find out if mental illness is becoming more of a health issue that is likely to affect older people in England.

COMMENT

If we consult statistical data about mental illness in England, we can conclude that mental health problems are affecting increasing numbers of the population. In 1992, 10 million prescriptions for antidepressants were administered in England online: **www.statistics.gov.uk**. *By 2007, this figure rose to just under 35 million prescriptions. This appears to indicate that mental illnesses like depression are becoming more of a problem for older people within England. Old age is frequently associated with declining physical health. It is also important to recognise that the ageing process may also link to deteriorating mental health. This can result in older people having complex physical, intellectual, emotional and social needs.*

Dementia

Cheston and Bender (2003, p46) have outlined how dementia is currently understood or 'formulated'. It can be argued that dementia is a generalised cognitive (information processing) and intellectual deterioration within the individual produced by 'brain dysfunction'. Whereas 'senile dementia' refers to a dementia syndrome that develops after the age of 65, 'presenile dementia' refers to the occurrence of dementia prior to the age of 65. The form of dementia that has become most popularised is known as Alzheimer's syndrome. Alzheimer's is a form of brain dysfunction named after its discoverer, Alois Alzheimer, in 1907. The disease causes changes in thinking and behaviour from 'normal' patterns to bizarre and disorientated confusion.

Individuals with Alzheimer's may act in confused, paranoid, tired or depressed ways. Sometimes they can appear 'normal' and in the early stages of the disease there is often denial of the condition. Personality changes such as depression, anxiety, inability to concentrate and denial may be the first signs of the beginnings of the disease. Memory loss is considered to be the major symptom and this may be the cause of many of the personality and behavioural changes we see in the early stages of the syndrome. From being 'absent minded', Alzheimer's develops to the point where the individual loses their memory for everything, including their own name. As a consequence daily life is likely to become chaotic and confusing.

At one time it was thought that Alzheimer's was synonymous with 'senility' and that everyone would suffer from the condition if they lived long enough. Now it is accepted as being a specific syndrome and not simply a consequence of normal ageing. Although the exact cause of the condition may be a matter of debate, authors such as Grey-Davidson (1999) draw attention to what 'facts' are known about Alzheimer's. It can be argued that at least five possible explanations might account for the origins of the syndrome:

- a deficit or imbalance of neurochemicals, particularly of an enzyme known as choline acetyl transferase. This enzyme is central to the production of acetyl choline, which is a neurotransmitter and thus of great importance to the normal functioning of the brain;

- excessive accumulations of toxins such as aluminium in the brain;

- there might be a genetic component in the development of Alzheimer's disease;

- a unique viral infection that does not show the usual symptoms such as a fever or a raised white blood-cell count, and therefore goes unnoticed and untreated;

- a significant decrease in blood flow to the brain, as well as a reduction in the amount of oxygen and glucose present in the blood.

Although it might not be possible to identify the precise cause of Alzheimer's what is conclusive is the effect the disease has on those who are affected by its consequences. This means that if you are going to work with older people in social services it is important to consider how you might make your professional practice as effective as possible. As we have already emphasised it is important to ensure that the wider skills of the multidisciplinary team are utilised so that holistic therapy that is a combination of health and social care is offered to older service-users.

ACTIVITY 6.8

What might be some of the difficulties that are likely to be experienced if you are working with service-users with Alzheimer's?

COMMENT

If you are working with service-users who have Alzheimer's it is important to remember that their 'cognitive map' is likely to be different from that of other people. This means that you may need to use alternative strategies for communicating. You may find that using simple repetitive language enhances interaction. Chapter 2 outlined the different methods of communication that are available to social workers. It may be the case that more awareness of non-verbal communication is necessary for service-users with Alzheimer's who are likely to become confused about verbal interaction. One suggestion is that your practice may benefit from considering alternative strategies of communication that utilise the interpersonal strengths of your service-users.

Intellect and old age

Many people perceive older people to be forgetful, unable to think clearly and repetitive in their storytelling. As we have seen in Chapter 3, many of our impressions of old age and of older people in general are based on inaccurate knowledge or social stereotypes. While it is true that certain sensory and motor abilities do decline with age, Horn and Donaldson (1976, 1977) have drawn attention to the 'myths' accounting for the supposed loss of intellectual faculties as one gets older. In other words do not assume that all older people experience a decline in cognitive ability as a result of age.

It may be assumed that as a person gets older, physical 'wear and tear' is combined with mental decline. Warner Schaie (1996) argues that the relationship between intellectual development and age is altogether more complicated. Machin (2000, p94) cites the work of Stephanie Clennell as evidence that old age does not equate to the loss of cognitive faculties. Studies such as Schaie's (1996) work break down the myth of intellectual deterioration during late adulthood.

Despite the potential of continued learning to guide our development throughout our adult lives, many of the celebrated accounts of learning (such as the work of Piaget and Vygotsky) are associated with learning in childhood as opposed to learning in old age. The researchers have tended to be especially interested in stages of learning in childhood and how peers influence this learning. The consequence of this trend is that it indirectly reinforces the presumption that older adults cannot continue to develop and grow cognitively.

ACTIVITY 6.9

What aspects of intellect do you think decline as one gets older? Can you think of any aspects of intellect that might improve with age?

COMMENT

We referred to Horn and Donaldson in Chapter 3 in relation to stereotypical attitudes towards older people. Their earlier work (1976, 1977) indicates that although memory, reasoning ability and mental attention span worsen as one becomes older there are aspects of intellect that become better with age. Some older people can notice that their verbal/conceptual ability improves with age. It also appears to be the case that mathematical ability improves with age. The final aspect of intellectual improvement that appears to improve with age is 'social awareness'. The explanation for the change in intellectual ability appears to be related to changes within the memory and these changes are considered in the next section of the chapter.

CASE STUDY

David has an acute anxiety about getting older. He is 65 and he used to be a headmaster of a school. He went to university and read English. He is depressed because he thinks that as he is approaching old age his physical and mental abilities will disappear. He believes in society's stereotypical views of older people. He tells you that at his grammar school the teacher used to use his answers at maths to mark the work of the other pupils and thinks this skill will go. He remembers school assemblies when staff and children listened to his views. His passion in life is cryptic crosswords but he worries that this ability will go too. What care plan would you develop to help David using Horn and Donaldson's work?

COMMENT

Horn and Donaldson (1976, 1977) contradict the stereotypical notion that old age leads to a reduction in intellectual ability. If verbal/conceptual/mathematical ability and 'social awareness' improve with age it can be argued that David has many skills that can be used effectively. David's care plan could be developed so that he is encouraged to interact with a local school as opposed to being alienated from the world of work. He could become a school governor or 'guest speaker' so that he is able to make an effective contribution to the school environment. This would also mean that he would feel more positive about himself and realise that approaching 65 does not necessarily mean the loss of intellectual ability.

Memory and ageing

It can be argued that there are three types of memory:

- sensory memory;
- short-term memory;
- long-term memory.

Sensory memory

'Sensory memory' refers to all of the sensory stimuli to which the individual is exposed. We are constantly being bombarded with sensory stimulation, particular that of a visual nature. Due to the amount of stimulation we receive, many of the impressions made by such stimulation can only be held in the brain for fractions of a second. After this time they leave the mind and they are soon replaced by new sensory impressions.

Short-term memory

'Short-term memory' can be described as the individual's immediate attention span. Sprenger (1999, p48) argues that although this type of storage is more selective than sensory memory, it is still quite limited in duration, lasting 30–60 seconds. Maintaining information in short-term memory is usually achieved through a process known as 'rehearsal'. For instance, finding a telephone number and remembering it long enough to make the call would involve the use of short-term memory. Most people tend to recite the number over and over in an effort to remember the digits. It would appear to be the case that we can retain information in short-term memory for between 30 and 60 seconds. In an early study in this area in the 1870s, Hermann Ebbinghaus found that he was able to memorise up to seven items in any one attempt, but if he tried to increase this number then it took much longer to memorise this additional information. Later work by George Miller in 1956 developed the Ebbinghaus findings. This led Miller to suggest that the capacity of short-term memory could be anything from five to nine items, and this became known as 'the magic number seven plus or minus two' (Miller, 1956). If this is the case, how are we able to remember information that is equivalent to more than nine items, for example a long telephone number? Miller proposed the idea of 'chunking'; if we can group the information to be memorised into a smaller number of meaningful or manageable chunks then it becomes within the capacity of short-term memory.

ACTIVITY **6.10**

1 *Look at the following sequence of letters for about 30 seconds: RA CFB IIR ANU TCI ARA FAA*

2 *Now see how many of these letters you can recall.*

3 *When you have done that, do the same thing with the following sequence of letters: RAC FBI IRA NUT CIA RAF AA*

4 *How did you do this time?*

According to Miller's work you are likely to have recalled more letters from the second group than from the first, yet the actual letters in both groups are the same. This is because the second sequence is 'chunked' into groups, many of which you will have come across in everyday life. This demonstrates that the capacity of short-term memory can be increased if the information to be remembered is arranged into meaningful chunks before it is memorised. These findings could be applied to social work by ensuring that older service-users have their short-term memory capacity assisted through 'chunking activities'. This might help them to recall some of the information that is no longer easily accessible in the short-term memory.

Long-term memory

In contrast to both sensory and short-term memory, long-term memory has an unlimited capacity and its duration can be anything from a few minutes to permanent duration. This particular memory store tends to hold all memories not currently being used, but which are potentially retrievable if and when necessary. The sorts of memories found in this store would be memory for language, objects, concepts, people and places and previously learned skills. For example, if you have learned to swim, ride a bike or to drive a car, these skills will be stored in long-term memory and only accessed when they are needed.

One way of passing information from short-term memory to long-term memory is through the process of rehearsal. In addition, it is also necessary to code the information so it can be placed into relevant categories in long-term memory, similar to postcoding mail in order to sort it into the correct pigeonhole.

Hayslip et al. (1982) have refined the idea that there is memory decline in older people by arguing that it is not so much that memory declines but more that it becomes harder to retrieve the information as one gets older. This has led to increasing interest in the ways in which information is memorised and subsequently recalled and applied. Brown et al. (2003, p114) discuss the processes operating between the brain and the mind. It can be argued that there are three main 'stages' involved in the memory process:

- acquisition;
- storage;
- retrieval.

Acquisition

This refers to our initial awareness of the information that will eventually form the memory. In other words we need to attend to and be aware of information before it can be stored either temporarily, for example a telephone number, or permanently, for example how to drive a car. This process of acquisition is described as being 'selective' because of the variety of complex variables influencing whether we remember a particular series of events.

Storage

The next stage involved in memory, 'storage', is the stage we tend to think of when we talk about 'memory', that is the information we have stored in the brain. Storage involves structural and chemical changes in the brain, creating a 'memory trace' which can be either temporary or permanent. As we have already seen, part of this process of creating a memory trace is very much dependent on 'coding' the information which has been attended to in the first instance. 'Chunking' is an example of such coding.

Retrieval

This third and final stage of memory involves accessing information previously stored in memory. No matter how attentive we are to our environment, and how much of the information within that environment we 'take in', this information will be of little use if it cannot be retrieved as and when needed. There are two general ways in which information can be retrieved from memory: 'recognition' and 'recall'. 'Recognition' involves matching a currently seen item, such as a photograph of a service-user, with a previous experience of how you worked with that particular individual. 'Recall' entails bringing information already stored in the memory into consciousness. 'Recall' would involve being able to provide a description of a particular service-user without any prompting or any photographs.

Draaisma (2004, p2001) applies the phrase that *life speeds up as you get older* in relation to the changes in memory processes with age. In other words older people are less able to recall and retrieve information. This suggests that coding and storage of information does not necessarily decline with age, but that it is the retrieval of information that deteriorates. The changing nature of memory in relation to age means that it is important to ensure that social workers working with older people need to be aware of what can be done to help improve the cognitive functions of older service-users. Poon et al. (1992, p129) draw attention to the importance of reminding older people to use memory strategies that have been learned and proven effective in the past so that these potential difficulties can be overcome.

ACTIVITY 6.11

How might Poon et al.'s suggestion be applied to the social worker/service-user?

COMMENT

If we try to apply Poon et al.'s work we would need to ensure that social worker/service-user interaction is holistic so that the social context of interaction is combined alongside other forms of therapy. We have already seen that encouraging older service-users to use memory strategies is one way of attempting to combine professional practice with psychological techniques. If this approach is implemented it may lead to a highly effective combination of health and social care practice.

It is important to ensure that we do not make stereotypical assumptions about older people in relation to cognitive abilities. Do not assume that because a service-user is old he or she will not be able to remember what you are saying. There are always likely to be service-users who do not have good memories, whether they are young or old, and this can have negative effects on the social worker/service-user relationship. What is especially important is the need to ensure that society's negative stereotypical images of older people are not reinforced through social work practice.

C H A P T E R   S U M M A R Y

This chapter has looked at the process of ageing. It is important to emphasise that the term 'older person' cannot be defined in terms of chronological age and that socio-historical and cultural factors need to be taken into consideration. The chapter has discussed some influential theories accounting for the ageing process. Wear and tear theory, cellular theory and immunity theory each draw attention to the physical processes of ageing. No one can deny the truism that the body gets physically older. Many external and internal bodily changes take place during the ageing process and these changes are reflected in the types of physical disorders that occur within the older population. Alongside being aware of these physical changes and the impact that they have on service-users it is also important to be aware that it is the social construction of old age within society that shapes attitudes to old age and in turn affects psychological welfare. Depression and dementia are conditions that are likely to affect older people so it is important for social workers to be able to apply specific strategies in order to work effectively with these service-users. The latter sections of the chapter have looked at intellect and memory in older adults. It can be argued that intellectual decline is not an inevitable consequence of the ageing process and that although Horn and Donaldson (1976, 1977) have drawn attention to a general decline in memory within older people this is more in relation to recalling memories as opposed to remembering information per se.

Self-assessment questions

6.1 Why is the wear and tear theory of ageing, considered to be inadequate in explaining the ageing process?

Briefly describe the cellular theory of ageing.

What are the three versions of immunity theory and how do they differ?

6.2 Is it true that intellect deteriorates with age?

6.3 Define the terms 'short-term' and 'long-term' memory.

Which of the following pieces of information do you think would be stored in short-term memory?

• childhood memories

• a telephone number immediately prior to dialling

• knowledge of how to drive a car

How much information can be held in short-term memory at any one time? How might this capacity be increased?

FURTHER READING

Gross, RD (2005) *Psychology: The science of mind and behaviour*, 5th edition. London: Hodder Arnold.
An excellent text in terms of depth and detail.

Malim, T, and Birch, A (2000) *Introductory psychology*. London: Palgrave Macmillan.
An accessible text that is applied to social care contexts.

Conclusion

This book has been written for social care workers who need to develop their skills in relation to applying academic concepts to professional practice. It can be argued that psychology provides a number of potential explanations for complex aspects of human behaviour. This is one of the reasons why the discipline is now an integral part of the social work syllabus. Each of the main chapters refers to the core elements of the recommended benchmarks for social work education as stipulated by the Department of Health. An aim of the book is to ensure that an emphasis is placed upon developing skills and knowledge that are relevant to effective collaborative working in relation to the development of good practice.

The book has taken into consideration the National Occupational Standards (NOS) for social workers. At the beginning of each of the main chapters the relevant standards are documented. These standards emphasise the importance of social workers being able to work effectively to meet the needs of individuals, families and communities. Indeed Crawford and Walker (2003, p123) maintain that the standards make it essential for social workers to ensure that their professional practice enables them to:

- prepare for work with people and assess their needs and circumstances;

- plan, carry out, review and evaluate practice;

- support individuals to represent needs, views and circumstances;

- manage risk;

- be accountable with supervision and support for own practice;

- demonstrate professional competence in social work practice.

It can be argued that if these standards are applied to social work practice some of the questions currently asked of the profession may be answered.

Book structure

The book has adopted an interactive approach by using activities and case studies so that psychology is applied to specific social care contexts. The book has also attempted to exemplify high academic standards by proposing analytical arguments in relation to other texts and authors. This enables a synthesis of academic argument in relation to practical social work concerns. 'Icebreakers' have been used in each of the main chapters in order to introduce a central theme contained within the subsequent pages. It is also hoped that this book is more than a general psychology textbook because the text places psychology within the everyday context of social work practice.

Each of the main chapters of the book concentrates upon a particular aspect of psychology in relation to social work. Chapter 1 began by referring to the analogy that exists between the painting of *The Ship of Fools* and the discipline of psychology. We may think of this social science subject as resembling an academic 'ship of fools' because of the uncertainty that has existed over the direction in which the discipline should move. In other words, whereas behaviourist psychologists such as Skinner have emphasised the importance of external environmental factors in producing thoughts, humanists such as Rogers have placed an emphasis upon the importance of unique individuals processing thoughts that have been generated by the environment in a highly original way. Which direction should the 'ship' move in? We answered this question by arguing that it is important to adopt a holistic approach to psychology if it is to be applied to social work as effectively as possible. In other words, we need to take into consideration the arguments of behaviourists, humanists, psychodynamic, cognitive and biological theorists in relation to social work practice. The therapies that are offered to social work practice from each perspective of psychology have merits that depend upon the type of service-user and the particular context within which the therapies are being applied. This chapter links to all three units of Key Role 1 of the NOS. By considering psychological perspectives and the therapies that are available to social workers we are *preparing for social work contact and involvement*. It can also be argued that consideration of the link between psychological ideas and social work practice can enable *individuals, families, carers, groups and communities* to make informed decisions. If the ideas of humanism are applied so that service-users are able to become empowered a key aim of social work practice can be achieved. It can also be proposed that the application of selected psychological therapies such as psychodynamic counselling can in certain contexts 'recommend a course of action' for particularly complex service-user needs.

Chapter 2 has explored the psychology of communication. It can be argued that good interpersonal skills are a requirement of high quality social work practice. It can also be suggested that good interpersonal skills can be the product of being aware of what leads to effective verbal and non-verbal communication. This chapter has considered the work of Juliet Koprowska (2005) in developing the argument of the importance of needing to be aware of interpersonal communication if effective social work practice is to follow. This chapter has links to all nine of the units of Key Role 1 of the NOS. If one has well developed communication skills it is possible to *respond to crisis situations*. Such skills also enable the practitioner to ensure that there occurs effective interaction with *individuals, families, carers, groups and communities* in order to facilitate the development of *life opportunities*. It is also the case that good communication skills are at the heart of effective care plans and that this in turn helps in meeting *assessed needs and planned outcomes*. Moreover, it can be proposed that effective interpersonal interaction is likely to help group work by *addressing behaviour which presents a risk to individuals, families, carers, groups and communities*.

Chapter 3 has discussed the link between attitudes, beliefs and behaviour. This chapter has given explanations for the occurrence of stereotypical attitudes and has explored the links between stereotyping and discrimination. It can be argued that the expression of discriminatory attitudes has become more complex in our increasingly technological world. This means that it is important to be aware of the psychological factors that lead to the formation of discriminatory attitudes. Discrimination may have always been an inevitable part of social life. It may always be a part of social life in the present and the future. Nevertheless, if our awareness of how discriminatory attitudes are formed is raised this may in turn heighten the awareness of how good social work practice can be put into effect. The chapter links to Key Role 3 of the NOS. If social workers are aware of the factors that cause prejudice and discrimination they are more likely to be able to be effective 'advocates' of others. It can also be argued that a heightened awareness of what constitutes good practice in relation to avoiding discriminatory attitudes will form the basis of what it is like to work effectively with others.

Chapter 4 has identified and discussed some of the explanations of mental illness. We have seen that it is wrong to argue that 'there is no such thing as mental illness' and that the Kesey (1962) notion of mental illness being nothing other than a form of social control is not a full and legitimate answer to the question *what is mental illness?* At the very least it is important to acknowledge that there are people with complex needs and that these needs are named 'mental health needs'. It can be proposed that good social work practice ought to ensure that as many positive ideas from psychology and other disciplines are applied in helping service-users with 'mental health needs'. The chapter has links to Key Role 5, Unit 17 of the NOS by raising awareness of effective working practice within multi-disciplinary teams. If social workers are aware of what professional help and assistance can be given by psychologists and psychiatrists it is more likely that these professionals will be included within the wider aim of meeting particularly complex service-user needs.

Chapter 5 has discussed the contribution made by psychology to understanding child development. As well as outlining the key arguments of celebrated psychologists such as Piaget and Vygotsky an emphasis has been placed upon the notion of 'the developing child'. The chapter has argued that it is particularly important that social workers are aware of the many varied factors that affect a child's development and that it is especially important to take psychological factors into consideration. This means that there is a link to Key Role 6, Unit 21 of the NOS because if social workers are aware of what psychological and other factors contribute to child development they are in turn contributing to the promotion of best practice.

The final chapter has discussed some of the contributions that psychology has made to raising awareness of the ageing processes. This chapter has referred to biological theories as well as applying cognitive theory and social learning theory to interpreting issues around old age. Any social worker who is to work with older people needs to know about the reality of old age as opposed to believing the stereotypical perception of what old age is supposed to be. This means that the chapter has links to Key Roles 1, 2, 3, 5 and 6. The chapter has reflected upon some of the ways in which effective work with *individuals, families, carers, groups and communities* can be achieved. It also has considered ways of *planning, carrying out, reviewing and evaluating* social work practice with older service-users. The chapter has suggested ways in which social workers can help older people to *represent their needs* alongside suggesting strategies for the effective promotion of 'support' for the social work practice of older service-users.

If we are to work effectively with older service-users we do need to ensure that there is professional competence in social work practice. This would be an ultimate aim of the book and a major theme running throughout each of the chapters.

Psychology may be a complex yet interesting subject. It may appear to be an academic 'ship of fools'. It can be suggested that it is when psychology is applied to social work that some of the true merits of the discipline can be seen.

Answers to self-assessment questions

Chapter 1

1.1 The five major schools of psychology are: psychoanalytical, behaviourist, humanistic, neurobiological and cognitive.

1.2 The best way of applying psychology to social work is through holistic therapies that combine the principles of behaviourism, humanism and cognitive, psychodynamic and neurobiological psychology to meet the complex needs of individuals.

1.3 See Table 1.

Table 1 *Answer to question 1.3*

School of thought	Strength	Weakness
Behaviourism	Acknowledgement of environmental influences on the mind	A tendency to neglect individual creativity with external factors
Humanism	Acknowledgement of how individuals manipulate external variables	Rogerian theory is idealistic
Psychodynamic	Acknowledgement of the workings of the unconscious mind	The theory is not methodologically proven
Cognitive	Acknowledgement of the different thought processes during human cognitive development	The idea of stages of development is not necessarily the case Cognitive development is more a process than a series of stages
Neurobiological	Acknowledgement of the link between human thoughts and hormones/chromosomes	The theory is biologically reductionist

Chapter 2

2.1 • Interpersonal communication is any communication that takes place between two or more people.
  • Vocal behaviour refers to aspects of speech, such as intonation, pitch and pauses.
  • Non-vocal behaviour refers to related behaviour such as communicating via clothes and eye contact.
  Vocal behaviour is exemplified by the ways in which social workers and service-users talk to each other.
  Non-vocal behaviour is exemplified by the ways in which social workers and service-users communicate by choice of clothes, body language, posture and eye contact.

2.2 The main channels of NVC are: gaze, facial expression, body position/posture and consistency.

2.3 Complementary transactions

   Crossed transactions.

   Ulterior transactions.

Chapter 3

3.1 Fishbein and Ajzen's (1975) 'Theory of Reasoned Action' states that measures of attitude and subjective norm can predict behaviour:

Attitude (A) + Subjective Norm (SN) = Behavioural Intention (BI)

3.2 The two main factors influencing attitude formation in the 'Health Belief Model' are:
- the individual's awareness of what threatens health;
- the individual's awareness of what behaviours are likely to reduce threats to health.

3.3 The three levels of oppression according to Thompson (1997) are:
- personal;
- cultural;
- structural.

Chapter 4

4.1 • Neurosis affects only part of the personality; psychosis affects the whole personality.

• Neurosis does not cause the sufferer to lose touch with reality; psychosis does.

• The neurotic recognises that there is a problem; the psychotic does not.

4.2 The psychoanalytic approach is a long-term process that focuses on past conflicts so that the service-user can work through their problems. Behavioural approaches aim to help the service-user to unlearn negative associations.

'Eclectic' therapeutic approaches use a combination of techniques to provide an all-round framework tailored to the service-user's specific needs.

4.3 The three main categories of psychotherapeutic drugs are:

- anti-anxiety drugs;

- anti-psychotic drugs;

- antidepressants.

Chapter 5

5.1 The main perspectives accounting for the development of the child's personality are behaviourism, humanism, psychodynamic theory, cognitive theory and biological psychology.

5.2 Malim and Birch (1998, p468) argue that both Piaget and Vygotsky accept the fundamental importance of the child interacting with its environment if cognitive development is to occur. The difference may be considered to be how the two psychologists are perceived. Whereas Piaget is characterised as placing an emphasis upon stages of cognitive development, Vygotsky is remembered for his notion of a 'scaffold' of influential peers influencing cognitive thought processes. It is important to acknowledge that although the two psychologists may have a difference in focus this does not necessarily mean that they are diametrically opposed to one another.

5.3 It can be argued that it is too simplistic to argue that a child's personality is a product of either its biology or its social circumstances. It is more effective to acknowledge that personality development is a complex combination of social, environmental and biological variables. This view is supported by writers such as Richard Gross (2004) who argue against reducing personality development to one particular set of variables.

Chapter 6

6.1 The wear and tear theory of ageing likens human beings to machines, which cannot repair themselves. It can be argued that it is too simplistic to liken human beings to 'machines'.

The cellular theory of ageing considers the way that errors in cell division throughout life contribute to degenerative diseases. The faulty cells affect and eventually impair the function of the body where they are found.

The three versions of immunity theory are:

- the theory that the immune system can no longer recognise slight deviations or faults in molecular structure and cell characteristics;

- the theory suggesting that even though the immune system can recognise 'deviations' it is not able to produce enough antibodies to destroy them. This means that the immune system can and does recognise faults in the molecular and cell structure but it is unable to overcome these faults;

- the 'auto-immune theory' suggesting that ageing is a result of the development of antibodies within the body that destroy not only abnormal cells but also those that are normal and healthy.

6.2 The notion of intellectual deterioration with age is more of a stereotypical perception than a reality. Malim and Birch (1998) reinforce the findings of Horn and Donaldson (1976, 1977) by emphasising that there are aspects of intellect that improve with age such as numerical ability.

6.3 'Short-term' memory is an individual's attention span. 'Long-term' memory stores all memories not being currently used but which are potentially retrievable.

Of the three examples, a telephone number immediately prior to dialling would be stored in short-term memory.

Approximately 30–60 seconds worth of information, or five to nine items, can be held in short-term memory at any one time. This capacity can be increased if the information is split into meaningful chunks.

References

Abelson, RP (1981) Psychological status of the script concept. *American Psychologist*, 36: 715–29.

Abraham Lincoln Quotations, 1 March 2006. (Online: **www.quotationspage.com/quote/29375.html**)

Adorno, TW et al. (1950) *The authoritarian personality*. New York: Harper.

Ajzen, I (1988) *Attitudes, personality and behaviour*. Milton Keynes: Open University Press.

Ajzen, I (1989) Attitude structure and behaviour. In SJ Brerckler and AR Pratkanis (eds) *Attitude structure and function*. Hillsdale, NJ: Erlbaum.

Ajzen, I and Fishbein, M (1977) Attitude-behaviour relations: a theoretical analysis and review of theoretical research. *Psychological Bulletin*, 84: 888–918.

Allport, GW (1935) Attitudes. In CM Murchison (ed) *Handbook of social psychology*. Worcester, MA: Clark University Press.

Argyle, M (1988) *Bodily communication*. London: Methuen.

Argyle, M and Colman, AM (1995) *Social psychology*. London: Longman.

Atkinson, RL, Atkinson, RC, Smith, EE and Hilgard, ER (1987) *Psychology*. Sydney: Harcourt Brace Jovanovich.

Audi, R (1995) *The Cambridge dictionary of philosophy*. Cambridge: Cambridge University Press.

Bandura, A (1977) *Social learning theory*. London: Prentice Hall.

Banyard, P (2002) *Applying psychology to health*. London: Hodder and Stoughton.

Bateson, G (1972) *Steps to an ecology of mind: Collected essays in anthropology, psychiatry, evolution and epistemology*. Chicago: University of Chicago Press.

Becker, E (1975) *The denial of death*. London: Macmillan.

Berne, E (1968) *Games people play*. Middlesex: Penguin.

Bernstein, B (1961) Social class and linguistic development. In AH Halsey, J Flaud and CA Anderson (eds) *Education, economy and society*. London: Collier-Macmillan.

Berry, DS (1990) 'The perceiver as naïve scientist or the scientist as naïve perceiver? An ecological view of social knowledge acquisition'. *Contemporary Social Psychology*, 14: 145–53.

Biebel, D and Koenig, HG (2004) *New light on depression: Help, hope and answers for the depressed and those who love them*. Michigan: Zondervan.

Binfield, M (2006) 'Lack of duty acts as barrier to social care support for homeless people', 2 February 2006. (Online: **www.communitycare.co.uk**).

Bowlby, J (1953) *Child care and the growth of love*. Harmondsworth: Penguin Books.

Bowlby, J (1969) *Attachment and loss: Vol 1 Attachment*. New York: Basic Books.

Bowlby, J (1973) *Attachment and loss: Vol 2 Separation anxiety and anger*. New York: Basic Books.

Bowlby, J (1988) *A secure base: clinical application of attachment theory*. London: Routledge.

Brown, A, Cocking, R and Bransford, J (2003) *How people learn: brain, mind, experience and school.* Washington, DC: National Academy Press.

Cheston, R and Bender, M (2003) *Understanding dementia: The man with the worried eyes.* London: Jessica Kingsley.

Chomsky, N (1972) *Language and mind*. New York: Harcourt Brace Jovanovich.

Clayton, V and Birren, JE (1980) Age and wisdom across the lifespan: theoretical perspectives. In PB Baltes and OG Brim (eds) *Lifespan and development*. New York: Academic Press.

Crawford, K and Walker J (2003) *Social work and human development*. Exeter: Learning Matters.

Davison, G, Neale, J and Kring, A (2003) *Abnormal psychology*. New York: Wiley.

Deaux, K and Lewis, L (1983) Components of gender stereotypes. *Psychological Documents*, 13: 25.

Draaisma, D (2004) *Why life speeds up as you get older*. Cambridge: Cambridge University Press.

Erikson, E (1995) *Childhood and society* London: Vintage.

Fazio, RH (1986) How do attitudes guide behaviour? In RM Sorrentino and ET Higgins (eds) *Handbook of motivation and cognition*. New York: Guildford Press.

Fishbein, M and Ajzen, I (1975) *Belief, attitude, intention and behaviour: An introduction to theory and research*. Reading, MA: Addison-Wesley.

Gardner, H (1985) *Frames of mind: The theory of multiple intelligence*. New York: Basic Books.

Geertz, C (1988) *Works and lives: The anthropologist as author*. Stanford, CA: Stanford University Press.

Golightley, M (2004) *Social work and mental health*. Exeter: Learning Matters.

Golightley, M (2008) *Social work and mental health*, 3rd edition. Exeter: Learning Matters.

Gottesman, II and Shields, J (1982) *Schizophrenia, the epigenetic puzzle*. New York: Cambridge University Press.

Grahame, K (1993) *Wind in the willows*. Hertford: Wordsworth Editions.

Grey-Davidson, F (1999) *The Alzheimer's sourcebook for caregivers*. Chicago: Lowell House.

Gross, R (1992) *Psychology: The science of mind and behaviour*, 1st edition. London: Hodder and Stoughton.

Gross, R (1999) *Psychology: The science of mind and behaviour*, 2nd edition. London: Hodder and Stoughton.

Gross, R (2004) *Psychology: The science of mind and behaviour*, 4th edition. London: Hodder Arnold.

Gross, R (2005) *Psychology: The science of mind and behaviour*, 5th edition. London: Hodder Arnold.

Guardian Online, February 2006. (Online: www.guardian.co.uk)

Hayslip, B, Kennelly, KJ and Maloy, RM (1982) Memory awareness in nursing home residents. *Canadian Journal of Psychiatry*, 36: 300–24.

Holliday, R (1995) *Understanding ageing*. Cambridge: Cambridge University Press.

Holmes, T and Rahe, R (1967) The social redjustment scale. *Journal of Psychosomatic Research*, II: 213–18.

Horn, JL and Donaldson, G (1976) On the myth of intellectual decline in adulthood. *American Psychologist,* 30: 701–19.

Horn, JL and Donaldson, G (1977) Faith is not enough: A response to the Baltes-Schaie claim that intelligence does not wane. *American Psychologist*, 32: 369–73.

Horn, JL and Donaldson, G (1980) Cognitive development in late adulthood. In Brim OG and Kagan (eds) *Constancy and change in human development*. Cambridge, MA: Harvard University Press.

Ingleby, E (2006) Reinventing Melchizedek: interpretations of traditional religious texts in the seminary context. In E Arweck and P Collins (eds) *Reading religion in text and context*. Aldershot: Ashgate.

ITV Lost for words, January 1999.

James, W (1995) *Immunisation: The reality behind the myth*. Westport, CT: Greenwood Press.

Johnson, M (2005) *The Cambridge book of ageing*. Cambridge: Cambridge University Press.

Kelley, HH (1973) The process of causal attribution. *American Psychologist*, 28: 107–28.

Kelley, HH and Thibaut, JW (1978) *Interpersonal relations: a theory of inter-dependence*. New York: Wiley Interscience.

Kesey, K (1962) *One flew over the cuckoo's nest*. London: Picador.

Klatz, R and Goldman, R (1997) *Stopping the clock*. New Canaan, CT: Keats Publishing.

Knapp, M and Daly, JA (2002) *Handbook of interpersonal communication*. London: Sage.

Koprowska, J (2005) *Communication and interpersonal skills in social work*. Exeter: Learning Matters.

La Piere, RT (1934) Attitudes versus action. *Social Forces*, 13: 230–7.

Linssen, H and Hagendoorn, L (1994) Social and geographical factors in the explanation of European nationality stereotypes. *British Journal of Sociology*, 23: 165–82.

Lippman, W (1922) *Public opinion*. New York: Harcourt Brace & World.

Lord, S, Sherrington, C and Menz, H (2001) *Falls in older people: Risk factors and strategies for prevention*. Cambridge: Cambridge University Press.

Machin, L (2000) *Women ageing: Changing identities challenging myths*. London: Routledge.

Malim, T and Birch, A (1998) *Introductory psychology*. London: Macmillan.

Malim, T and Birch A (2000) *Introductory psychology*. London: Macmillan.

McGuire, WJ (1989) The structure of individual attitudes and attitude systems. In Brerckler and AR Pratkanis (eds) *Attitude structure and function*. Hillsdale, NJ: Erlbaum.

Metchnikoff, E (2000) *The evolutionary papers of Elie Metchnikoff*. Dordrecht: Kluwer Academic Publishers.

Miller, GA (1956) The magic number seven plus or minus two: some limits to our capacity for processing information. *Psychological Review*, 63: 81–97.

Online dictionary. (Onlne: **www.dictionary.reference.com**)

Parsons, T (1967) *The structure of social action*. New York: Free Press.

Pennington, D et al. (2002) *Introducing psychology: Approaches, topics and methods*. London: Hodder and Stoughton.

Plath, S (1963) *The bell jar*. London: Faber and Faber.

Plunkett, K (1981) Psycholinguistics. In B Gilliam (ed) *Psychology for today*. London: Hodder and Stoughton.

Poon, LW, Rubin, D and Wilson, B (1992) *Everyday cognition in adulthood and late life*. Cambridge: Cambridge University Press.

Richards, G (2002) *Putting psychology in its place*. London: Psychology Press.

Rogers, C (1961) *On becoming a person*. Boston: Houghton Mifflin.

Rosenstock, IM (1966) Why people use health services. *Millbank Memorial Fund Quarterly*, 44: 94–124.

Rutter, M (1981) *Maternal deprivation reassessed*. Harmondsworth: Penguin.

Samuel, M (2006) Care services failing older people. (Online: www.communitycare.co.uk)

Saunders, AR and Gejman, PV (2001) Influential ideas and experimental progress in schizophrenia genetics research. *Journal of the American Medical Association,* 285: 2831–3.

Schaie, KW (1996) *Intellectual development in adulthood: The Seattle longtitudinal study*. Cambridge: Cambridge University Press.

Scheff, TJ (1966) *Being mentally ill*. Chicago: Aldine.

Skelt, A (1993) *Caring for people with disabilities*. London: Pitman.

Skinner, BF (1957) *Verbal behaviour*. New York: Appleton-Century-Crofts.

Slater, R and Gearing, B (1989) Attitudes, common stereotypes and prejudice about ageing. In B Gearing, M Johnson and T Heller (1989) *Mental health problems in old age: A reader*. Chichester: John Wiley & Sons.

Sprenger, M (1999) *Learning and memory: The brain in action*. Rosewood, MA: Association for Supervision and Curriculum Development.

Stainton-Rogers, W (1991) *Explaining health and illness: An explanation of diversity*. London: Prentice Hall.

Starr, B and Weiner, M (1981) *The Starr-Weiner report on sex and sexuality in mature years*. New York: McGraw-Hill.

Steele, JG, Treasure, E, Pitts, NB, Morris, J and Bradnock, G (1998) Total tooth loss in the UK in 1998 and implications for the future. *British Dental Journal*, 189(11): 598–603.

Telegraph Online, 12 May 2006. (Online: www.telegraph.co.uk)

Thompson, N (1997) *Antidisciminatory practice*. Basingstoke: Macmillan.

Toates, F (2000) *Biological psychology: an integrative approach*. Upper Saddle River, NJ: Prentice Hall.

Watson, A (2004) Reconfiguring the public sphere: implications for analyses of educational policy. *British Journal of Educational Studies*, 52 (3): 228–48.

Winston, R (2003) *The human mind and how to make the most of it*. London: Bantam.

Wynne, LC, Singer, MT, Bartko, J and Toohey, ML (1977) Schizophrenics and their families: research on parental communication. In JM Tanner (ed) *Developments in psychiatric research*. London: Hodder and Stoughton.

Zajonc, RB (1968) Attitudinal effects of mere exposure. *Journal of Personality and Social Psychology*, 2: 1–27.

Zimbardo, PG (1979) *Psychology and life*. Glenview, IL: Scott Foresman.

Index

Added to the page reference 'f' denotes a figure and 't' denotes a table.

LAURENCE ANHOLT has created more than 200 books for children which are published in 30 languages. His self-illustrated Anholt's Artists series have sold millions of copies around the world, including *Camille and the Sunflowers, Degas and the Little Dancer, Leonardo and the Flying Boy, Picasso and the Girl with a Ponytail, The Magical Garden of Claude Monet, Tell Us a Story, Papa Chagall* and *Cézanne and the Apple Boy*. Laurence has also collaborated on numerous picture books with his wife, the artist Catherine Anholt. Their titles have won many awards, including the Nestlé Smarties Gold Award on two occasions. Laurence's first Young Adult novel, *The Hypnotist* is published in October 2016. The Anholts live and work in a house on a hill above the sea in Devon.

With love for Anna Bugg, who inspired us all.

JANETTA OTTER-BARRY BOOKS

First published in Great Britain in 2016 by Frances Lincoln Children's Books.
This paperback edition first published in Great Britain in 2017 by Frances Lincoln Children's Books,
74-77 White Lion Street, London N1 9PF
QuartoKnows.com
Visit our blogs at QuartoKnows.com
Text and illustrations copyright © Laurence Anholt 2016

A catalogue record for this book is available from the British Library.

ISBN 978-1-84780-667-3

Illustrated with watercolours

Set in Chimp and Zee and Bentham

Printed in China

Photographic Acknowledgements

Please note: the pages in this book are not numbered. The story begins on page 6.

Paintings by Frida Kahlo © 2015.
Banco de México Diego Rivera Frida Kahlo Museums Trust, Mexico, D.F./DACS.

Page 7 above left: Portrait of Engineer Eduardo Morillo Safa, 1944,
Fundacion Dolores Olmedo, Mexico City. © 2015 Photo SCALA, Florence

Page 7 above right: Portrait of Lupita Morillo Safa, 1944, Private Collection

Page 7 below: Portrait of Alicia Morillo Safa and her son Eduardo, 1944, Mexico City. © 2015 Photo SCALA, Florence

Page 8: Portrait of Doña Rosita Morillo, 1944, Fundacion Dolores Olmedo, Mexico City. © 2015 Photo SCALA, Florence

Page 13: Frida Kahlo: Self-Portrait with Monkeys, 1943. Photo: akg-images

Page 30: Portrait of Mariana Morillo Safa, 1944, Private Collection

Page 31: Photograph of Frida Kahlo in San Francisco, 1939. Photo: akg-images

135798642

Frida Kahlo

and the Bravest Girl in the World

LAURENCE ANHOLT

Frances Lincoln
Children's Books

There was once a girl with big brown eyes. Her name was Mariana.

She lived in a house in Mexico, full of paintings by a famous artist named Frida Kahlo.

Frida had painted Mariana's daddy.

Frida had painted her big sister, Lupita.

Frida had painted her mum and her brother, Eduardo.

But Mariana's favourite painting was of her wise granny, Dona Rosita. Frida Kahlo had painted every white hair on the old lady's head, so the painting seemed almost alive.

"I want to be painted too!"
said Mariana.

"You are too little," said her big sister.

"You could never sit still, Mariana," said Dona Rosita. "Frida made me sit for so long I knitted three scarves and a pullover."

"Anyway, Mariana would be scared to go to Frida's house," teased her brother. "It's full of strange paintings and **Frida keeps a skeleton above her bed.**"

Mariana's eyes grew big and wide.

But one day Mariana's daddy said, "Mariana, now it is your turn. You can go to Frida's house on Saturday."

Mariana felt very nervous as she rang the bell at the Blue House.

She waited a long time.

She thought about the strange paintings and the skeleton.

At last the door opened and there stood Frida Kahlo....

She was as beautiful as a Mexican princess!

Frida wore rings on her fingers
and flowers in her hair,
and a beautiful dress
which reached right to the floor.

"Hello, kid," said Frida.
"How are you doing?"

"I'm a little scared,"
said Mariana.

"Well, that's
OK," said Frida.
"Everyone feels
scared sometimes.
Now take my hand
and let's go inside."

If Frida was a
princess, her house was
like a bright blue
fairytale palace.

Frida did not have children, but she had lots of animals.
"Come and meet my friends," she said.

"This is Fulang Chang, my spider monkey.

This is Bonito, my parrot.

This is my favourite little dog.
He's called Mr Xoloti."

"What a funny name!" said Mariana.

"This is my baby deer, Granizo.

And this is my beautiful eagle,
Gertrude Caca Blanca."

"What does Gertrude Caca Blanca mean?"
asked Mariana.

"Hey, kid," laughed Frida.
"Don't you know?
It means Gertrude White Poo!"

Mariana almost laughed.
But she was still a little frightened.

"Listen, Little Sister," whispered Frida.
"If you are very lucky you will meet my favourite friend of all.
He's an ugly Frog-Toad, **as big as an elephant.**"

Mariana's eyes grew big and wide.
She knew that princesses liked frogs. But she
hoped she wouldn't have to kiss him.

"You and me are going to be pals," said Frida.
"Let's go to my studio, little Mariana."

Frida walked very slowly, with a
stick in one hand. They went into
the studio filled with Frida's
paintings - the pictures were
strange but they were
very beautiful.

"OK, kid, let's get to work," said Frida.

Mariana sat in a tall chair.
Her feet didn't even touch the ground.

Mariana tried to sit still.
She looked at all the funny
things in the studio - toys and
candy and dolls.

"Frida, where is the enormous Frog-Toad?" she asked.

"Oh, he'll hop along at lunchtime," said Frida.
"My Frog-Toad is always hungry."

They sat in the sunshine and ate delicious food.
Mariana gave a banana to Fulang Chang. Frida gave
some apple to Granizo.

Then the gate opened and someone came
into the yard.

Mariana felt scared.
She saw an enormous man with a
fat tummy and **big froggy eyes.**

Frida gave the man a kiss. "Mariana, meet Diego, my favourite Frog-Toad. Diego, this is my friend, Mariana. I'm painting her today."

Diego smiled and kissed Mariana's hand. Then he ate the biggest meal that Mariana had ever seen.

"Diego is a great painter," said Frida. "Maybe the greatest painter in Mexico."

"And my Frida is **the greatest painter in the world,**" said Diego.

After lunch Frida said, "I'm too tired to paint any more. I need to rest a while. Help me to my bedroom, Little Sister."

Mariana remembered what her brother had said.

"I think I'll go home now," she said.
"I don't like skeletons."

"You are a funny kid!"
laughed Frida.

There was Frida's bed and on top of the bed was - **the skeleton.**

But this skeleton was not scary at all!

It was a big toy skeleton with a funny hat and a silly smile on its face.

Frida rested while Mariana looked at her colourful clothes in the wardrobe.

"I love your dresses," she said.
"Thanks, kid," said Frida.
"You know why I wear a long dress all the time?"

"Because you are a princess," said Mariana.

Frida laughed. "Listen, Little Sister, come and sit beside me
and I'll tell you a true story...

...When I was a kid I went to school in the city.

One day I got on a bus with a boy..."

"Was he your boyfriend?" asked Mariana.

"Yes, he was my boyfriend," laughed Frida.

"Anyway, a dreadful thing happened. The bus was in a crash with a tram.

It was a terrible accident. They put me in hospital for a long, long time."

"Poor Frida. Did it hurt?"

"It did hurt, kid. It hurt me then and it hurts me now.
It hurt so bad they had to make a special plaster coat to hold
my body still. They carried me home and put me in this bed.
I was dead scared, Little Sister.
I thought my life was over."

"But it wasn't over, was it, Frida?"

"No way, kiddo. I was just beginning. One day my papa
made me a special easel and gave me some paints.

He even fixed a mirror above my bed. 'Look up
there, Frida,' he said. 'That's the bravest girl
in the world.'"

"And that's when you started painting!"

"You've got it. I said to the funny skeleton, 'Listen, Boney, Frida may be broken, but she sure ain't finished. I'm never going to be scared of anything again. I'm going to be a painter. I'm going to be a better painter than any man in Mexico!'"

"And if it wasn't for the accident, you wouldn't be an artist!" said Mariana.

"Maybe that's true. The doctors told me I would never walk again, but **no one** tells Frida what to do! Slowly I learnt to walk, but I always wore long dresses to cover my broken leg."

All week Mariana waited for Saturday so she could go to the Blue House.

Mariana loved Frida and Frida loved Mariana.
She told her lots of funny things to make her laugh.

"Look here, Little Sister. Have you ever seen anything like it?"

Hanging on the line were three pairs of pink
underpants, big enough for an elephant.

"They belong to Diego!" giggled Frida.
"He's so big, he has them specially made!"

But sometimes Frida had to paint in a wheelchair.

Mariana felt very sad for Frida. But Frida said,

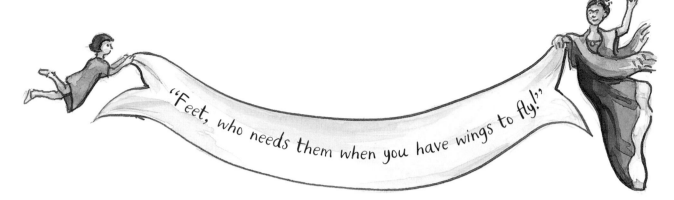

"Feet, who needs them when you have wings to fly!"

"We are stronger than we think, Mariana. And here's a little secret - women are stronger than men.

It's true!

Diego is a huge enormous Frog-Toad, but he's really like a big baby. Did I tell you that he plays with toys in his bath? I am only small, Little Sister, and I suffer all the time, but in my heart I am stronger than any man alive."

Frida gave Mariana lots of presents - a special little chair so that Mariana could reach the ground. And her own baby skeleton with a hat. Mariana looked at the skeleton and she said, "Listen, Boney. I'm the bravest girl in the world."

Then one Saturday, Frida said the painting was finished.

"Let me see! Let me see!" called Mariana.

Frida only smiled.

She wrapped the painting in brown paper and tied a ribbon around it.
She told Mariana to open it at home.

"Your granny, Dona Rosita, is a wise old woman.
If she likes the painting, then it can't be too bad. But listen, Mariana -
I have painted a name at the bottom of the picture.
It is the name of the **strongest,**
bravest,
most beautiful little woman I know."

"Of course," said Mariana, "You have signed your name -
FRIDA - on the painting. No one is braver than you."

Mariana said goodbye to the animals.

And when she kissed Diego, the big Frog-Toad, she pretended
she didn't know about his pink underpants or his bath toys.

Frida had one last present for Mariana -
a Mexican princess dress, just like hers!

"Promise me you'll be strong like me, Little Sister.
Promise me you will fly in your life."

Mariana kissed Frida and hugged her hard and promised that she would.
Then she took her daddy's hand and walked out of the Blue House.

"Well," said Granny Dona Rosita.

"Can we see your painting?"

Everybody gathered around as Mariana untied the ribbon.

There was the girl with the big brown eyes, sitting perfectly still on her own special chair.

Dona Rosita said it was the most beautiful painting in Mexico.
And she should know - she's a very wise old lady.

And underneath was the name of the
strongest, bravest girl in the world.

Frida Kahlo

Frida Kahlo was born on 6th July, 1907, in the house known as Casa Azul, the Blue House, in Coyoacan, Mexico. She was adored by her German father, who was a photographer, and her mother, who was of Mexican Indian descent. She had three sisters and two half-sisters. Although she developed polio when she was eight, Frida was a bright and feisty girl, who loved playing practical jokes.

Frida grew up at a time of political unrest and later developed a passion for Communism, which stayed with her for life. In 1922, Frida enrolled at one of the best schools in Mexico with the aim of going into medicine. However, at 18 years of age, all her plans were turned upside down when she was involved in a terrible accident. A tram crashed into the bus on which she was a passenger, and Frida sustained near-fatal injuries. She spent a month in hospital and throughout her life she suffered acute pain in her spine and leg, leading to more than 30 operations.

While she was recuperating in a plaster cast, her father, Guillermo, gave her a set of oil paints and she began to express herself through art.

When she was able to walk, Frida showed her work to the great Mexican muralist, Diego Rivera, who encouraged her to continue as an artist. Frida fell in love with her 'ugly frog-toad' and in 1929 they were married. In many ways, they made an unlikely couple but they shared a love of art, Communism and a wild and spontaneous sense of humour. Later Diego and Frida separated, but they could not live apart. They remarried and, after the death of Frida's parents, moved into the Blue House where Frida, who was unable to have children, surrounded herself with a menagerie of animals.

Frida's reputation as an artist grew, especially in France and America, and she also became famous for her flamboyant sense of fashion, such as her long Tehuana dresses and elaborate hairstyles. She particularly loved the earrings in the shape of hands, given to her by Picasso.

Frida was befriended by a wealthy art lover, the engineer, Eduardo Morillo Safa, who collected her work. In 1944 Morillo Safa asked Frida to paint six members of his family including his youngest daughter, Mariana. Frida adored children and they became great friends. Frida gave Mariana many gifts, including the little chair she used for her portrait, and she even had a small Tehuana dress made for Mariana. Mariana said, 'I loved her and she loved me and petted me all the time.'

Their friendship endured for the rest of Frida's life, and Mariana was present in 1953 at Frida's first major show in Mexico City. Frida was gravely ill and one leg had been amputated, so her doctors told her that she would not be able to attend the opening night. Stubborn and determined to the end, Frida ordered an ambulance and her bed was carried into the middle of the gallery, where Frida entertained the adoring crowd, dressed in her finest Tehuana dress.

Frida Kahlo died, aged 47, on 13th July, 1954, in the Blue House in Coyoacan. The Casa Azul is now a museum and a shrine to Mexico's greatest artist who continues to inspire, not only through her powerful paintings, but through her determination and irrepressible spirit. Frida Kahlo is lovingly remembered as a unique artist, a champion of human rights and a feminist icon.

MORE BOOKS IN THE ANHOLT'S ARTISTS SERIES

For over 20 years, the Anholt's Artists series has introduced readers to some of the world's most famous artists through the real children who knew them. Telling inspirational true stories and featuring reproductions of the artists' work, these titles bring art to life for children everywhere.

Anholt's Artists Activity Book
978-1-84507-911-6

Leonardo and the Flying Boy
978-1-84780-816-5

Camille and the Sunflowers
978-0-71122-156-7

Matisse, King of Colour
978-1-84780-043-5

Cézanne and the Apple Boy
978-1-84780-604-8

Picasso and the Girl with a Ponytail
978-0-71121-177-3

Degas and the Little Dancer
978-1-84780-814-1

Tell Us a Story, Papa Chagall
978-1-84780-339-9

The Magical Garden of Claude Monet
978-1-84780-813-4

"A great introduction to art . . . highly recommended."
– *The Observer*

Frances Lincoln titles are available from all good bookshops.
You can also buy books and find out more about your favourite titles,
authors and illustrators on our website: www.franceslincoln.com